his purpose Our privilege

A CHRISTMAS DEVOTIONAL

Other Books by Tifainé Hedgecock

Empty Chairs, A memoir of Monday Supper
The Girl Who Grew A Gallery, A children's story set during the Covid-19 Pandemic

His Purpose Our Privilege

Contents

Dear friend,

I've written this book to fit within the Advent season and lead up to Christmas day. As the first Sunday of Advent is four Sundays before Christmas day, unless December 25th is a Sunday there will always be less than seven days in the last week of Advent. Nevertheless, I chose to make this book four complete weeks, so depending on which year you read this you may finish after Christmas Day.

Each week has a theme: Hope, Faith, Joy and Peace. Each daily reading should take less than a few minutes to read. Each day has a Scripture passage with it, some questions to think about, room to doodle, and a prayer.

The things I've written are intended to lead on one to the next, but if you miss a day don't feel you can't move on to 'today' until you've caught up. I see more value in spending *some* time with God than none at all. If the pressure to 'catch up your reading' before you can go on overwhelms you, please accept my permission (if it's needed) to just skip right to where you want to be. Likewise, if you're still reading this in March, that's okay. Perhaps we should be thinking about Christ's birth every day of the year. Or perhaps you can give yourself permission to lay this aside, and bring it out with anticipation and joy next Advent. Do what works for you. I wrote this for you (yes, you) and one of the last things I would like to think is that it becomes a burden. Please be kind to yourself.

At the end of the week there is a page called 'If this is all you have time for this week.' This could be helpful if you are reading this book as a group and you feel have to cram all your reading into the few minutes right before your group meets. It's like a cheat sheet.

When you can, allow space and time for God to meet you while you think about what you've read, whether that's straight-away or while you're loading the dishwasher. It's Christmas. Give yourself the gift of thinking about your saviour.

When you see a poinsettia like this at the bottom of a day's reading, it's a short prayer I wrote for you to use. Use it as it is, or as a creative springboard for your own conversation with God. For now, I'm going to conclude this intro with the prayer I'm praying today and all through Christmas.

Love, *Tifaine*

God, thank you for the privilege of writing this book. I hope the words on these pages help someone understand a little more about the story of your beloved son's birth. I hope the words on these pages soothe someone or give them insight they previously didn't have. I have faith that you, my all-powerful God who can use all things for our good and your glory, will be with all those who read this. Thank you for the joy you gave me while I was writing. I pray that these words bring joy to others. Bring peace to our communities and our families, dear Lord; bring the real peace that you're known for: reconciliation, restoration and wholeness. I would love to think that someone comes to know your grace and forgiveness through these words, so when that happens, Lord, please help them get connected into a lovely church community where they can love and be loved. Amen.

hope

May the God of hope fill you with all joy
and peace as you trust in him, so that you
may overflow with hope by the power of
the Holy Spirit.

ROMANS 15: 13

Day 1

What is hope?

While the word used as hope is just another word for expectations or desires, we most naturally associate hope with desires for positive things.

If we call someone hopeful, we typically mean they are optimistic: she hopes she'll be offered the job, he hopes this treatment works. Additionally, of course, this positive outcome will be at some time point in the future. We don't need to hope for what we already have. The child who has sneaked into her mother's wardrobe to see what Christmas gifts might be hidden there may hope the toy she sees is hers; when the same child unwraps that toy from under the tree some weeks later, she no longer needs hope.

Many of the things we hope for are not that distinct from the gifts children hope to open on Christmas day. Where a child wishes for toys and games they think they will enjoy, likewise we hope for things we think will bring us happiness. Where a child wishes for products they have seen advertised so we too might hope for things we believe will make us feel better, or might bring us comfort, reduce our workload or alleviate our loneliness.

Despite being told we can have peace or other wonderful feelings we might feel our life is neither peaceful nor wonderful. We may be experiencing illness or financial hardship, relationship discord, confusion, tension or conflict. We may be experiencing several of those things at once.

> WHEN WE CONSIDER OUR LACK IT CAN SEEM TO BE EVIDENCE THAT EVERYONE IS LIVING THEIR 'BEST LIVES' EXCEPT US

At some point in the past we may have hoped life would look a certain way by a certain time, but that time point passed by and life still looks the same. When we consider our lack it can seem to be evidence that everyone is living their 'best lives' except us.

Published studies show that hopelessness is a strong predictor for suicide and suicidal thoughts, even when the researchers take into account other factors such as depression or acute devastating events. It seems that without hope we literally find it hard to live. The thought that we are in a harrowing situation with no possible likelihood of change creates responses in us that can overwhelm us to the point we are no able longer think clearly. Yet, with hope, we are able to endure immense hardship, imprisonment, debilitating illness, lasting pain and huge losses.

The fact that bookshop Christmas displays, viral social media videos and TV biopics produce the stories of people 'just like us' who withstood extraordinary challenges imply we love a good story of hope being proven right.

As hope looks ahead to the future it inherently features risk: we might not get what we hope for. Or we must decide how long we will continue to hope for. Hoping for the good things God promises is always worthwhile, but even then our hope doesn't guarantee things will turn out exactly as we envisage.
We are reminded that overflowing with hope, and being filled with joy and peace while we hope, is possible, not by wishful thinking or because of a positive attitude, but by the power of the Holy Spirit.

Today's scripture calls God 'the God of hope.' We are reminded that overflowing with hope, and being filled with joy and peace while we hope, is possible, not by wishful thinking or because of a positive attitude, but by the power of the Holy Spirit.

Do you consider yourself
a hopeful kind of person?

What kind of things do
you hope for?

Is there anything you've
been hoping for that you
feel you've been over-
looked about?

Prayer
Almighty God, At the start of this
Christmas season, we remember that you
are the God of hope. May we overflow with joy
and peace by the power of your Spirit. Amen.

For to us a child is born, to us a son is given, and the government will be on his shoulders. And he will be called Wonderful Counsellor, Mighty God, Everlasting Father, Prince of Peace. Of the greatness of his government and peace there will be no end. He will reign on David's throne and over his kingdom, establishing and upholding it with justice and righteousness from that time on and forever. The zeal of the Lord Almighty will accomplish this.

ISAIAH 9:6-7

Day 2

God's love and faithfulness established hope

In the ancient Hebrew scriptures (what we call the Old Testament) we read of God speaking to his people in a variety of ways, but often through key people we call prophets: for example Moses, Samuel, Isaiah, Jeremiah, or Elijah.

From Sunday school we might remember their history: how Abraham's family began with Sarah, how the twelve tribes of Israelites became a nation. Again and again they were told they were a special people group chosen by Yahweh. As a nation they flourished. The Israelites looked and acted differently to their neighbours and they worshipped a God that had no image or statue. Although they didn't look like fearsome warriors, they were formidable opponents. The power of their God was renowned. God's love for his people and his faithfulness to them meant they were constantly protected and provided for in miraculous ways. Reports of the miracles that accompanied the exploits of the tribes of Israel spread to all the neighbouring nations.

One of their first kings and best leaders was called David. Not only was he celebrated as a skilled warrior, but King David was also celebrated for his closeness to God who called him 'a man after my own heart.'[1] At the end of David's life, it was the prophet Nathan who prophesied that one of David's descendants, someone from the tribe of Judah like him, would one day come to establish his family line forever.

Despite this prophecy, however, with each successive king the Jewish people fared less well. The kings they had didn't worship God as David had and the tribes fought among themselves until their kingdom was divided. The two kingdoms were eventually conquered and the people were taken off as captives. This once feared nation was now scattered and seemingly abandoned.

GOD CONTINUED TO SPEAK TO HIS PEOPLE AND ESTABLISHED WAYS FOR THEM TO REMEMBER HIM

Despite this, God continued to speak to his people and established ways for them to remember him. In the hopelessness of defeat and captivity, prophets reminded the people of the character of God. Some of the verses you might hear the most at Christmas come from the prophet Isaiah. The prophets preached hope: God will one day send someone to rescue them.

So, they waited.

The prophets had spoken about the hope of rescue but

no evidence of a rescuer coming. God had said he would send someone to deliver them, to establish a government, to reign over them.

Then, the prophecies stopped altogether. There is a gap from where the Hebrew Bible chronicles end and where the Christian Scriptures (what we call the New Testament) begin in which there are no prophetic visions or messages from God. Hundreds of years of silence after generations of promises.

Still, generation after generation they waited.

Just like us waiting for the things we hope for, some days the Jewish people might have been content to rest in God's plan and God's timing, other times they were desperate to take matters into their own hands, and yet other times they may have wondered whether they were remembering correctly at all.

If God said he would send someone to conquer our enemies, then where is our deliverer? Is the notion that God would send us a deliverer just a children's story? Should we give up? Are we irrational to have a hope we will rescued? Have we dreamed up this whole thing?

Is God still with us? Is God even real?

Now they had a choice: maintain their hope and keep waiting or give up their hope and do what they wanted. It seems they did a bit of both. Corporately, they believed God had a plan for his people. Individually people started having their own ideas of what deliverance might look like or how it might be accomplished.

Just like us, when we're comfortable we behave one way; when things get painful, we tend to start looking for ways to make the suffering stop.

Through their shared history God had laid the foundations for their hope. Through their religious practices God gave them ways to remember his character. Each of their religious festivals showed some aspect of God's faithfulness to them in the past and pointed to his promise for their deliverance in the future. But still, each person had to choose to believe the prophecies they'd heard. Each individual had to choose whether to keep up their religious practices and show who they worshipped, choose whether to remember that their God had always been faithful to them. They had to choose whether or not to live like a people of hope.

We face similar choices today.

> Yes, my soul, find rest in God; my hope
> comes from him.
> PSALM 62:5

Is being hopeful easy for you?

Have you ever hoped for
something for such a long
time you started to lose
hope?

Can you imagine a time
when you might be tempted
to stop hoping?

Prayer
Almighty God, we remember your
promises to your people all those thousands
of years ago and how you were faithful to fulfil
them. We think of your great love for us and ask you
help us to remember you are still faithful. Amen.

In the time of Herod king of Judea there was a priest named Zechariah, who belonged to the priestly division of Abijah; his wife Elizabeth was also a descendant of Aaron. Both of them were righteous in the sight of God, observing all the Lord's commands and decrees blamelessly. But they were childless because Elizabeth was not able to conceive, and they were both very old. Once when Zechariah's division was on duty and he was serving as priest before God, he was chosen by lot, according to the custom of the priesthood, to go into the temple of the Lord and burn incense. And when the time for the burning of incense came, all the assembled worshipers were praying outside. Then an angel of the Lord appeared to him, standing at the right side of the altar of incense. When Zechariah saw him, he was startled and was gripped with fear.

But the angel said to him: "Do not be afraid, Zechariah; your prayer has been heard. Your wife Elizabeth will bear you a son, and you are to call him John. He will be a joy and delight to you, and many will rejoice because of his birth, for he will be great in the sight of the Lord. He is never to take wine or other fermented drink, and he will be filled with the Holy Spirit even before he is born. He will bring back many of the people of Israel to the Lord their God. And he will go on before the Lord, in the spirit and power of Elijah, to turn the hearts of the parents to their children and the disobedient to the wisdom of the righteous—to make ready a people prepared for the Lord."

Zechariah asked the angel, "How can I be sure of this? I am an old man and my wife is well along in years." The angel said to him, "I am Gabriel. I stand in the presence of God, and I have been sent to speak to you and to tell you this good news. And now you will be silent and not able to speak until the day this happens, because you did not believe my words, which will come true at their appointed time.

LUKE 1:5-20

Day 3

Intellectual hope versus inspired hope

It had been about 450 years between when the Jewish people had last heard from one of God's prophets and when the story of Jesus' birth began. During this time, the people in began to divide into groups based around how they interpreted the scriptures. People had got used to living with what was written in the law without a prophet to teach and interpret for them.

By the time we start reading about Mary and Joseph and the birth of Jesus, the Jews were no longer captives, but they were subjugated to the Roman Empire who ruled the whole area. King Herod was appointed by Rome for ceremonial reasons and to keep the Jews orderly. The Jewish people under Roman rule practised their faith and followed the laws they'd been given but they held on their prophecies too. They held onto the hope that they would not be dominated forever but that a king would rise up among them who would rescue them from their enemies. The hope of a deliverer was ingrained into their culture through the reading of the scriptures and through their religious festivals.

One day, an old priest called Zechariah is on duty at the temple in Jerusalem. While he was burning incense as an act of worship and symbolic of the prayers of the people, he was visited by the angel Gabriel. As a priest, we would expect Zechariah to be able to recall and know scriptures related to the Messiah better than most, yet when the angel explains that his son will be the messenger to tell of the coming Messiah, the words out of his mouth convey disbelief. As a result of his disbelief, he is rendered mute.

Zechariah, a righteous and faithful priest had intellectual hope but also expressed doubt and confusion. Thirty years later we read about a woman at a well who, when questioned by the adult Jesus about her life, demonstrates a certain intellectual or philosophical hope herself. Without knowing she is talking to the Messiah, her answers show her intellectual knowledge of a future hope without any expectation it could be in progress now. Despite showing her knowledge that a messiah, an anointed saviour, was her people's future hope, she clearly wasn't expecting him to turn out to be standing in front of her. This woman showed she had hope in some mysterious better future, without allowing her life to be shaped by that hope. She had an attitude of 'things will be better tomorrow.'

Whether an upright priest working out his calling in a temple or a downtrodden woman in the grip of her life choices, both knew a messiah was coming but neither was expecting him.

THEY BOTH KNEW A MESSIAH WAS COMING BUT NEITHER WAS EXPECTING HIM

Zechariah's muteness which lasted until his son was born served as a witness to others. Everyone realised Zechariah had seen a vision and, as this was undoubtedly rare and the muteness astonishing, we can assume people would have talked about it. As Zechariah communicated (non-verbally, obviously) to the rest of his priestly cohort everyone had the chance to know the Messiah was coming.

The Samaritan woman at the well brought up the coming Messiah as a deflection. Jesus confirmed that was who he was by declaring, 'I, the one speaking to you—I am he' and she ran off to tell everyone in her village, a transformational event.[1]

Following their encounters, both Zechariah and this woman drawing water at the well would each have a profoundly new appreciation of the power and purpose of God. They were able to replace their intellectualised hope with inspired hope.

---

1   John 4:26

Are there things that you acknowledge intellectually or dispassionately but haven't yet fully internalised as hope for you personally?

Examples might be knowing God loves us but living as if we have to earn his approval, or knowing we are forgiven of all our sins but still feeling worthy of punishment

Have you ever known 'of' something but failed to grasp that it could be applicable to you?

Prayer
Father God, Some things in the
Bible seem difficult to understand. Some
things we know from your Word seem difficult
to remember when we're out in the world. Help us to
internalise the truth and live like the beloved children
we are. Amen.

Only be careful, and watch yourselves closely so that you do not forget the things your eyes have seen or let them fade from your heart as long as you live. Teach them to your children and to their children after them.

DEUTERONOMY 4: 9

Day 4

Reasoned hope

If we're hoping for something we don't have (and we agreed on the first day we can only hope for something we don't yet have) we must decide if we carry on hoping or if we stop. If we decide to go on hoping we must decide how we will live while we're hoping, how we will act while we don't have what we desire.

We can hope we get a certain job or a pay rise. We can hope the treatment works. We can hope there's not a disaster waiting for us when we get home where the dog has pulled everything out the garbage and chewed the sofa. We can hope that a certain someone notices how fabulous we are. But generally, there's not a lot we can do about those hopes. Some hopes we have we can control and some we cannot.

The hope we're talking about this week is the hope in a promise that was given by God to his people. God had repeatedly proven himself trustworthy and demonstrated his miraculous power to his people. The Jews documented their history, and in so doing, the miracles they had witnessed, and God commanded them to continually tell their children.

Don't we so easily forget things, even the amazing things? Don't we so often allow our present feelings or the opinions of those around us influence what we think? God knows this about us as he knows our nature. In this scripture today, God tells his people to 'watch themselves' so they don't forget. Because their children and grandchildren will not have seen the miracles and wonders, God commands that they be told. He implores his people to not let the truths they've seen and heard fade from their heart.

Hope takes courage and never more so than when the thing we're hoping for is personally important. Maintaining hope takes courage too, perhaps because as we go longer and longer without seeing the resolution of our hope, we can get fatigued. Like running a marathon, maintaining hope takes stamina. Depending on who we have around us we can even be persuaded to give up hope in our dreams. Well-meaning friends who don't want to see us disappointed or hate seeing us struggle can persuade us to create smaller hopes.

The Jews weren't hoping in something of their own imagination. They were hoping in something promised to them by their God. They hoped in something promised to them by the one who had proven faithful time and time again to their ancestors.

We cannot change our circumstances by positive thinking. It's not possible. However hard we think, we cannot get the grass to cut itself. We don't have control of stuff in that way. Hope is not saying 'If I just believe such-and-such hard enough then it will definitely happen.'

We know that God has the power to do or change or create anything, and it's good to hope for good things. It is pointless to hope for something that goes against God's character as God cannot sin and will not sin for us. When we hope for things consistent with His Word (healing, restorations, provision, to name a few) we are assured we are heard by God but it still doesn't mean we will get what we want the way we expect or when we expect. The prophets had hope in certain events given to them by God but in many cases, they didn't see the outcomes during their lifetimes. If we are given a specific word of hope from God we should keep believing for it, but it would be foolish to think that the only way our hope could be realised is the picture in our own imagination.

WE KNOW GOD HAS THE POWER TO DO OR CHANGE OR CREATE ANYTHING

The hope of a Messiah for God's people wasn't a hope the Jews thought up themselves, they didn't simply decide one day they didn't like their lives and so started hoping for a better one. The hope of the Jewish people was the hope in the fulfilment of a promise their ancestors had been given by God himself.

Despite receiving this promise from God, despite having hope passed on them from generation to generation, as time went on, and no deliverer came, no anointed one showed up, and as the time since God last reminded them of the promise got longer, so the source of the hope became more critical.

What promises of God
do you have trouble to
remember?

How can you 'watch
yourself' so you don't
forget?

Are any of your hopes
attempts to control God or
people, or not in keeping
with God's character?

Do you have specific plans
for how you want your
hopes to materialise?

Prayer
God Almighty, Help us remember
that you are God and we are not. Help us
to hope for things that are truly ours to hope
for and are in keeping with your perfect nature. We
trust that you have our best interests in mind and are
always working for our good. Help us remember your
goodness to us in the past. Amen.

But the angel said to her, "Do not be afraid, Mary; you have found favour with God. You will conceive and give birth to a son, and you are to call him Jesus. He will be great and will be called the Son of the Most High. The Lord God will give him the throne of his father David, and he will reign over Jacob's descendants forever; his kingdom will never end."

"I am the Lord's servant," Mary answered. "May your word to me be fulfilled." Then the angel left her.

LUKE 1:30-33, 38

She will give birth to a son, and you are to give him the name Jesus, because he will save his people from their sins.

MATTHEW 1: 21

Day 5

Results of hope

We read earlier that an angel called Gabriel told Zechariah he would have a son, and that same son would go on to prepare people for the coming of the anointed one, the Messiah.

We might imagine God whispering to Zechariah's heart. Have hope, Zechariah. I have a purpose on earth and I'm calling you to be part of it. That Messiah everyone's expecting? I'm choosing your son to get everyone ready. Your son will herald his arrival.

When Gabriel visits Mary a few months later, he tells her the miracle baby she will conceive will have attributes of the waited for Messiah. Have hope, Mary.

I have a purpose on earth and I'm calling you to be part of it. That deliverer that you've heard people talk about? That ruler to take over David's throne and lead Yahweh's chosen people? You're his mother.

The angel who visited Joseph in his dream when he was struggling with the news of his wife-to-be's pregnancy told him that Mary was carrying the saviour. Have hope, Joseph. I have a purpose on earth and I'm calling you to be part of it. The plan you've heard about through the writings of the prophets and the readings in the temple? That plan for a deliverer for my people? My plan is unfolding. The baby Mary carries will save people from their sins.

Zechariah and Elizabeth had a purpose: to raise John in keeping with ways of their faith.

John had a purpose: to preach repentance and remind people the Messiah was coming.

Mary and Joseph had a purpose: to raise Jesus as a fully human baby, full human child and fully human teenager.

After she accepted her assignment, Mary's recorded words are, 'I am the Lord's servant.' By Joseph's actions immediately and, then later when he protected Jesus from King Herod following the visit of the Magi, we can see he accepted and embraced his purpose to care for Jesus. We have prayers and praises recorded from Zechariah and Elizabeth that point to their full acceptance of their assignment from God. These four upright and righteous men and women stepped into the roles that God gave them and considered it a privilege to serve him.

THESE MEN AND WOMEN STEPPED INTO THE ROLES GOD GAVE THEM AND CONSIDERED IT A PRIVILEGE

Before these events occurred, I doubt Mary, Joseph, Elizabeth or Zechariah might have guessed they would be used as part of God's plan for the deliverance of his people. Mary might have considered herself too young, Elizabeth may have written herself off as too broken, Zechariah may have thought his usefulness was over, Joseph may have been fully occupied mapping out how his life would look—perhaps none of them considered they could be used by God in his incredible redemption story.

Do you discount yourself
from being used by God to
make his name known?

Are you fixed in your ideas
for how you believe you
might be used by God?

Prayer
Heavenly Father, May we have a
heart like Mary who quickly chose to
serve you even at cost to herself. Help us to
open our minds to all kinds of ways we might
serve you in our world. Help us not to restrict the
ways we imagine we might serve you. Amen.

I pray that the eyes of your heart may be
enlightened in order that you may know the
hope to which he has called you, the riches
of his glorious inheritance in his holy people,
and his incomparably great power
for us who believe.

EPHESIANS 1: 18

Day 6

A greater hope

Based on the writings of their prophets, we know the Jews had the hope that one day a deliverer would come to save them from oppression. The assumed the enemies from which they would be delivered were the current human rulers. For the deliverer, they imagined a warrior like King David with the priestly attributes of Aaron. They modelled Jesus after the scriptures they read, but also the attributes of the ancestral heroes they liked best. Perhaps Mary and Joseph too imagined Jesus would be a warrior like Israel's former kings: strong and might in battle, fearless and shrewd in their dealings with others. Often, our minds can't help imagining what future things will be like. I wonder if Mary and Joseph had questions as Jesus became an adult and didn't behave like a politician or a militant leader.

Mary and Joseph got to see their hope made flesh, but perhaps it wasn't quite what they imagined. Those who had a clear expectation that their deliverer would be a warrior to physically overthrow their rulers became more confused as the adult Jesus' public ministry gained momentum. Jesus showed no desire to lead a rebellion to take over the governance of Israel. Some of the elements of Jesus' purpose that he mentioned included 'to seek and to save the lost' and 'to preach' and 'to fulfil the law.' Hardly warrior attributes. Still, any confusion they may have had while he was alive paled next to the disappointment and confusion once Jesus was killed.

The privilege of being part of God's plan for the redemption of the world brought Zechariah humiliation when he couldn't speak for a while, Elizabeth joy, Joseph confusion, Mary scorn and, then later, grief. Fulfilling God's purpose brought Jesus himself degradation and death.

THE PRIVILEGE OF BEING PART OF GOD'S PLAN FOR THE REDEMPTION OF THE WORLD BROUGHT ZECHARIAH HUMILIATION AND BROUGHT MARY SCORN

At the garden of Gethsemane, just hours before he would be executed, Jesus reminds himself as he prays that his death is the purpose for which he came to earth. Despite the suffering death will bring him, Jesus tells his father, 'Not my will, but yours be done.'[1]

Despite Jesus himself telling his followers while he was alive that he needed to die, no one really understood. Not only was Jesus' birth prophesied in their scriptures, but so also was the whole of God's plan, including his son's death. After his resurrection, one of the first

---

1   Luke 22:42

things Jesus did was explain all the scriptures to his followers. Jesus' purpose was greater than anyone imagined. Jesus only fulfilled some of the prophecies during in his years on earth in the first century, the remainder we wait for still.

We who live after Jesus' birth, death and resurrection have the new hope that one day he will come again. Part of the tradition of Advent is that, in addition to thinking about the birth of Christ, we also think about when Jesus will come back to defeat all the evil in our world. At Jesus' second coming everything will be made new. That is our actual hope. We can identify with the first century Jews who waited for the birth of their Messiah as we wait for his coming again.

In the letter we call Ephesians in the Bible, we read a prayer for the believers at the time. Of all the things the writer could have prayed for, he desires they will know the unequivocal hope they have in Christ and the glorious richness they stand to inherit as children of God. Given the persecution endured by Christ-followers in the first century and the poor conditions of many, if we were in this writer's place, perhaps we would be praying for material blessings and healings and greater freedoms. Instead, we read how thankful he is for them and see him go on to pray exclusively for spiritual blessings together with a profound knowledge of the truth.

Having hope for the future is important, but hope in the wrong thing will only serve to disappoint us. Placing our hope in the future possession of a material object or another human being is false hope. False hope always fails us. The God of hope has the power to give us what we really need and all the joy, peace and strength we need to withstand hardship.

How do you feel when God's working in your life doesn't look like what you expected or imagined?

What thoughts come to mind when you consider that we are waiting for Jesus' second coming in a similar way to the Jews waited for his birth?

How do you feel about this prayer from Ephesians being about the believers' spiritual welfare rather than their present physical needs?

Prayer
Lord God, Help us understand the importance of our spiritual needs, and trust you completely for all our physical needs. Thank you that Jesus was obedient to you even to his own death. Help us understand your purposes in our lives and in our world so that we might join you working towards them. Amen.

His father Zechariah was filled with the Holy
Spirit and prophesied: "Praise be to the Lord,
the God of Israel, because he has come to his
people and redeemed them. He has raised up a
horn [meaning a strong king] of salvation for
us in the house of his servant David (as he said
through his holy prophets of long ago), salvation
from our enemies and from the hand of all who
hate us— to show mercy to our ancestors and to
remember his holy covenant, the oath he swore
to our father Abraham: to rescue us from the
hand of our enemies, and to enable us to serve
him without fear in holiness and righteousness
before him all our days. And you, my child, will
be called a prophet of the Most High; for you
will go on before the Lord to prepare the way for
him, to give his people the knowledge of salvation
through the forgiveness of their sins, because
of the tender mercy of our God, by which the
rising sun will come to us from heaven to shine
on those living in darkness and in the shadow of
death, to guide our feet into the path of peace."

LUKE 1: 67-79

Day 7

It's a privilege to tell others about our hope

Rather than happening as soon as his son was born, Zechariah's speech is only restored once he is named John at the ceremony. Whatever he might have felt, Zechariah's first recorded words after his voice was restored were praise to God. Zechariah delights in the centuries-old hope being realised: the God he has dedicated his life to is ready to send the Messiah.

I like to think Mary was there at this ceremony and heard Zechariah speak. Since she went to visit Zechariah and Elizabeth when she was in her first month and Elizabeth was in her sixth month of pregnancy and since Luke tells us (v.56) she stayed three months, I think maybe the timing works out. I don't know, of course, but I like the idea. Amid any fears and while she processed the hurtful questions and comments she'd probably heard, I like to think Mary had faithful friends in Zechariah and Elizabeth who loved her.

As Zechariah was a priest, I like to imagine he was kind enough to show Mary the scriptures of the prophecies of the Messiah. After his experience in the temple and a lifetime of reading the scriptures, I'm sure he had the knowledge if only he could find a way to make himself understood without his voice. I like to think he believed Mary straight-away when she said she'd been visited by Gabriel because he had been too. He knew the purpose of the Messiah and might have considered it his privilege to share his revelation with Mary, as she now carried that precious baby.

If Mary did hear his words, I imagine they would have helped. While she carried the baby in her body for six more months, giving up her dignity and her reputation to be part of God's redemptive plan for humanity she might be able to recall Zechariah's words of hope.

At the naming ceremony, reinvigorated with hope, Zechariah's exuberant reminder of the coming saviour's purpose would surely have given fresh hope to everyone listening. He boldly took the first opportunity he had to remind everyone what the Messiah would do: rescue them from enemies, make a way for them to serve God without fear, make them holy in God's sight. He doesn't waste a moment.

In Zechariah's prophesy we also notice his joy that his son will share the good news of what the coming Messiah will do. Whether or not Zechariah gets to see it, he knows his son will. John, who will go on to the called John the Baptist (or John the Baptiser) will remind people that hope is coming and what that hope can do. John will tell people about salvation, tell them that their sins can be forgiven by God.

What a special job God gave him! Like John, we also have the job of telling people what Jesus came to do. In a letter Paul writes to the Roman

LIKE JOHN, WE ALSO HAVE THE JOB OF TELLING PEOPLE WHAT JESUS CAME TO DO

believers some years after Jesus' resurrection, he tells them it is a privilege to tell everyone what God has done. The goal, Paul writes, is that others will believe too. The title for this Christmas devotional comes from that phrase in this passage. Telling others about Jesus and how he's changed our lives is a privilege given to us by God. If we believe that God's love and Jesus' sacrifice for us is truly life-changing, then wouldn't we want the people we know to learn of it?

> Through Christ, God has given us the privilege and authority as apostles to tell Gentiles everywhere what God has done for them, so that they will believe and obey him, bringing glory to his name.
> ROMANS 1:5 NLT

Yes, we should show Jesus by our actions, that is, by how we love those around us and how we live, but we also get to tell. Later in this same book Romans, Paul reminds us that people who don't know of Jesus can't call out to him.[1]

While we know that people can discover Jesus by watching how we live our lives, this usually entails spending a lot of time with them. By spending

---

1   Romans 10:14b

extended periods of time with others allows them to see our actions and behaviours across many situations. But who spends a long time with someone without hearing the name of their best friend? Who spends hours and hours working alongside someone and hear what they think? People who spend time with us should not only see us living lives that imitate Jesus but they should also hear his name.

As soon as Zechariah could speak, he told the people around him about the Messiah. Despite the fact they most likely already knew about the prophecies of Jesus, Zechariah didn't leave it to chance. The angels were so thrilled Jesus was born they told everyone who was awake. Once the shepherds had seen Jesus they told everyone they met. When John grew up his lifestyle would display his Nazarite beliefs to everyone, but he still chose to speak about the Messiah who was coming. It's a privilege that we are entrusted to tell this message of the hope to be found in Jesus and it's an act of love to help people discover hope for themselves.

Who encourages you and helps you keep following the voice of hope?

Do you have a 'Zechariah' in your life to help keep you hoping? Are you a 'Zechariah' to someone?

How easy or difficult do you find it to share the hope of Jesus with people? Is it easier to tell strangers or to tell friends?

Prayer
Lord God, May we be like Mary and seek out wise Christ-followers to encourage us. May we be like Zechariah and Elizabeth and encourage those around us while pointing to you. Show us ways to share the hope we have in Jesus with other people. Amen.

If this is all you have time for this week...

HOPE FOR A RESCUER What we see with our eyes here is not all there is. A few thousand years ago the Israelite nation had a hope given to them by God that a deliverer would come to save them. Their hope came from promises God had given them through their ancient prophets. To greater and lesser extents individuals held on to the hope they had been given and waited for some future time when 'life would be better.' As a people living under the rule and regulation of foreign powers, they hoped for their trouble and suffering to end so they could be free.

WHAT WE HOPE FOR The Jewish people hoped for rescue, and they imagined it looking a very specific way. We might have hopes: hopes for healing, hopes for relationship reconciliation, hopes for rescue, hopes that certain life circumstances improve, and, just like the first-century Jews, we can have very fixed ideas on what the solution might be. We can get stuck in imagining only one way of resolution.

A KINGDOM WITHOUT A FLAG The baby whose birth we celebrate at Christmas wasn't the warrior overthrower the Jews expected. When he grew up he didn't lead a rebellion and the kingdom he established didn't have a map or a flag. He didn't inspire a revolt against their foreign rulers but a revolt against unloving practices and idolatrous behaviours. Many Jewish people were so focussed on expecting a warrior deliverer coming to establish a new earthly kingdom that they missed the truth Jesus came to share.

HOPE OF JESUS Jesus preached hope: the hope of the kingdom of God, the hope of healing, the hope of freedom from anything that traps us, the hope of life after death, the hope of a permanent home with our heavenly father. The Jewish priests taught that we had a sinful nature and couldn't please God without regular sacrifices. Jesus confirmed this, but then gave himself as the ultimate and forever sacrifice so that we could be made blameless in God's sight. This is the deliverance that Jesus brings.

HOPE FOR REAL Like the first-century Jewish people we can also get confused with what hopes looks like and what things might bring us true peace or joy or freedom.

We have hope because God made a way for us to be forgiven and free.

We have hope because we are saved and made right with God through Jesus' life, death and resurrection.

We have hope because we know one day the trouble and suffering on earth will be over, Jesus will defeat evil and we can live in wholeness together with God.

OUR HOPE IS TOO GOOD NOT TO SHARE Zechariah considered it a privilege that his son was chosen to be the messenger going ahead of the Messiah. The apostle Paul, writing to the Romans in the first century, tells us God gives us the privilege to tell everyone what God has done and bring glory to his name.[1]

It's a privilege to tell others about the hope we have in Jesus

---

1   Romans 1:5

Faith

"I am the Lord's servant," Mary answered.
"May your word to me be fulfilled."
Then the angel left her.

LUKE 1: 38

Day 1

What is faith?

If hope is looking forward to something, perhaps faith is the belief that it's possible.

We hope to get that new job and have faith in our match for the required skills and experience. We hope a certain treatment will cure an illness and have faith in the drugs and medical personnel who have developed the treatment. In our earthly lives, however, neither of these scenarios guarantee success. When we are one of many equally qualified candidates, we may not be the one chosen for the job. Medication doesn't always result in a perfect cure, and sometimes diseases progress unpredictably. Our own abilities and strengths have limits so, faith in our own (or any other human's) abilities and strengths will also have limits.

The things we have faith in often turn out to be inadequate. Faith in God, on the other hand, is different. Faith in God is dependable.

God is infinite and unchanging, all-knowing, all-powerful and present everywhere at once. Our faith isn't in God doing things the way we think he should, or in our circumstances turning out the way we imagine they will: faith in God is believing he is who he says he is.

GOD IS INFINITE AND UNCHANGING, ALL-KNOWING, ALL POWERFUL AND PRESENT EVERYWHERE AT ONCE

Chapter 11 of the book of Hebrews is often called the faith chapter because so many verses begin with "By faith…". The chapter lists many characters from the Old Testament scriptures who served God and lists some of the things they did. If we were to go back and read their stories, we would find that each one worked under the belief that by doing the things God told them to do, deliverance or blessing or justice would come. But the last verse of the chapter reads 'These were all commended for their faith, yet none of them received what had been promised, since God had planned something better for us so that only together with us would they be made perfect.'[1]

Putting ourselves in their place, and imagining ourselves interpreting God's instructions the way we tend to, these men and women died without seeing God fulfil his promises. But, when we read the stories from our standpoint here 2000 years after Jesus birth, we can see how each one fits into the plan God had for his people. We can see how each generation, each faithful follower, took a turn in progressing the story that would lead to the birth of Jesus.

The deliverance their stories were working towards was not merely the conquering of a city or the rescue of some families in a certain area (although in many cases this was achieved). The deliverance they hoped for was yet to come and it would only come many generations later in the form of a baby born in Bethlehem. One reason I think their faith is commended is that their faith was entirely in the one who promised deliverance. They all had faith that the One who asked them to build a boat or demand freedom from an Egyptian Pharaoh or march around a city with their army seven times was trustworthy. They believed he was worth believing in. They had faith in the power, authority, goodness and trustworthiness of God.

So, when we speak of faith it should not be in getting what we want but in the God who says 'nothing is impossible.'[2] Our faith should not be in seeing the outcome we imagined but in the God who says he will work all things together for our good and his glory.[3] We have faith in the God who created all things, who is unchanging, who is good, who loves, who sees and knows more than we do. The One who is faithful to us even when we are faithless.[4]

Faith isn't a feeling, it's a decision to trust. God was consistently faithful to his people. Story after story after story in the Bible testified to his people how he protected them, provided for them and fought for them. Even when his people repeatedly acted poorly, he never abandoned them or changed his allegiance.

The prophets never saw the fulfilment of their prophecies during their lifetime, yet they had faith to keep on because they had faith in the one who gave them the words.

The prophets didn't rely on what they saw with their eyes, they

2   Luke 1:37, Matthew 19:26
3   Romans 8:28
4   2 Tim 2:13

remembered how God had shown up for them in the past and used that as fuel to remain faithful. These prophets pleased God by their faith not by the outcome of their actions. We can't do anything to impress God—he made us and he is the sovereign king over all creation. If we want to please him we offer the only thing we have—our choice to put our faith in him. Even if we manage to do the noblest of things, if we don't have faith in the character and power of God we are working in our strength and that's not what pleases him. We can't please God if we don't have faith in him.[5] We please God by putting our faith in him.

> Let us draw near to God with a sincere heart and with the full assurance that faith brings, having our hearts sprinkled to cleanse us from a guilty conscience and having our bodies washed with pure water. Let us hold unswervingly to the hope we profess, for he who promised is faithful.
> HEBREWS 10:22-23

---

5   Hebrews 11:6

What kind of things do you put your faith in? Are they all as reliable as each other?

Have any things ever proved themselves to be unworthy of the faith you gave them?

Prayer
Heavenly Father, Thank you that you are all-powerful and unchanging. When I put my faith in the wrong things, you are always faithful. Help me grow in my faith   in you, and reveal your character to me more and more so I can grow closer to you. Amen.

The angel went to her and said, "Greetings, you who are highly favoured! The Lord is with you."

Mary was greatly troubled at his words and wondered what kind of greeting this might be. But the angel said to her, "Do not be afraid, Mary; you have found favour with God. You will conceive and give birth to a son, and you are to call him Jesus. He will be great and will be called the Son of the Most High. The Lord God will give him the throne of his father David, and he will reign over Jacob's descendants forever;

his kingdom will never end."

"How will this be," Mary asked the angel,

"since I am a virgin?"

The angel answered, "The Holy Spirit will come on you, and the power of the Most High will overshadow you. So the holy one to be born will be called the Son of God. Even Elizabeth your relative is going to have a child in her old age, and she who was said to be unable to conceive is in her sixth month.

For no word from God will ever fail."

"I am the Lord's servant," Mary answered. "May your word to me be fulfilled." Then the angel left her.

LUKE 1: 28-38

Day 2

Reasoned faith

When Mary was visited by the angel Gabriel, he didn't ask her to do something in the same way Noah was asked to build an ark or Abraham was asked to leave his home, instead, she was told something would happen to her. Mary would have known she was not pregnant, nor could she possibly be, so this announcement certainly required some kind of next step. Unlike Zechariah who asked, 'How can this be?' (answer: God is can do anything) Mary asked, 'How will this be?' which I interpret more as a 'what should I do next' type question. As it turns out, Mary doesn't need to do anything as she is told the baby will be conceived by the Holy Spirit.

Mary shows astounding acceptance as she fully yields to be used in God's service. It was Mary's faith in who commissioned her, God, that enabled her to be completely obedient and willing to accept that all the practical details would all be taken care of.

We know that following the angel's visit Mary next went to see Elizabeth. Staying with Zechariah and Elizabeth for three months allowed her to process her situation among godly people who would protect her physically and spiritually. We know nothing about Mary's own parents, but with a potential deficit of role models, Mary was wise to go to see people who she could trust for support as she stepped out in faith. When we are without good spiritual support elsewhere, it is wise to seek out Christ-followers a step ahead of us in the journey so we can ask for guidance.

Once news of Mary's pregnancy became common, people might have asked her 'Did God really say you were to be the mother of the saviour?' or 'My husband told me that the Messiah would be born in Bethlehem, but here you are in Nazareth, so, the baby can't really be from God, can it?' When we hear peculiar news, we often can't help to ask questions or offer our opinions without stopping to consider how our words might affect others.

When Mary was faced with negative comments, persistent questioners, or even her own feelings, Mary would need to rely on what God had said to her through the angel. Mary would need to rely on her own faith that God was real, that God was trustworthy and that God would meet all her needs just as he'd met her ancestors' needs from the earliest days.

In the not too distant future, Mary would have physical signs of her pregnancy along with the certain knowledge she was a virgin. Perhaps these two apparently opposing facts would serve to augment her faith, but the immediate answer Mary gave to the angel after she'd been commissioned would need to be her over-and-over-again answer. Each time fear arose, or each time neighbours, family or friends spoke critically to her: "I am the Lord's servant.' And, perhaps, God Most High, I put my faith in you. I am willing to serve you. I trust you can take care of every detail. I'll just be here, doing what you told me, growing a baby.

How easy do you find it to seek
out help? How long do you wait
before you ask?

When faced with an assignment
that you believe is from God,
how easy do you find it to trust
him with the details?

How easy would you find it to
accept an assignment from God
if you knew it would certainly
turn your life upside down,
or require you to give up your
dignity?

Prayer
Most High God, help build my faith and
confidence in you and who you are so that any
negative comments or actions from others don't cause
me to give up serving you. Amen.

This is how the birth of Jesus the Messiah came about: His mother Mary was pledged to be married to Joseph, but before they came together, she was found to be pregnant through the Holy Spirit. Because Joseph her husband was faithful to the law, and yet did not want to expose her to public disgrace, he had in mind to divorce her quietly. But after he had considered this, an angel of the Lord appeared to him in a dream and said, "Joseph son of David, do not be afraid to take Mary home as your wife, because what is conceived in her is from the Holy Spirit. She will give birth to a son, and you are to give him the name Jesus because he will save his people from their sins."

All this took place to fulfil what the Lord had said through the prophet: "The virgin will conceive and give birth to a son, and they will call him Immanuel" (which means "God with us").

When Joseph woke up, he did what the angel of the Lord had commanded him and took Mary home as his wife. But he did not consummate their marriage until she gave birth to a son.

And he gave him the name Jesus.

MATTHEW 1:18-25

Day 3

Not all who wonder are faithless

Scripture tells us that Joseph was faithful to the law, and from his actions, it seems he's a good man overall. Yet, when told by the girl to whom he is betrothed to be married that she's pregnant but still a virgin he seems to doubt her honesty. His wife-to-be insists she became pregnant by the Holy Spirit coming upon her but that seems implausible. Despite his religious faith, he doubts what's going on is from God.

Different theologians have come up with different words to label the opposite of faith (certainty, unbelief, faithlessness), but most don't call it doubt. Interestingly, many of the people we know from prominent stories in our Bible questioned God and were still used by him. Israel as a nation wavered frequently between faith in God and faithlessness, between faith that their God would be enough for them and the belief their faith might be better placed somewhere else. But God never ever abandoned his people. Our faithlessness may sometimes lead us to a place far away from where we expected to be but God who is faithful waits with us. Our behaviour may take us to a place where we feel far from God, but he is always ready to welcome us back.

We have three verses in the gospel of Matthew to read about how Joseph. We learn that Joseph was a righteous man and faithful to the law. We are told he knew he should divorce Mary but his character meant he thought to do it quietly and without drama. We learn that while he had not yet started the process of divorce, he was thinking about it. Next, we read that, after the angel had visited him, Joseph decided to go ahead with the marriage but felt it wouldn't be appropriate to sleep with Mary until after Jesus was born.

REGARDLESS OF JOSEPH'S FEARS AND DOUBTS, GOD SAW HIS FAITHFULNESS

Joseph clearly had reservations about Mary's story. We can infer that even if she told him all that the angel Gabriel told her, Joseph doubted Mary's truthfulness or the plausibility of the story, or both. Rather than punish him for his doubt, God sends a messenger to Joseph too and grants him the privilege of also being told the name God wants for his son. Joseph is reminded the name means Yahweh Saves and told Mary's baby will save God's people from their sins.

It's probably safe to say that Joseph was not hoping that his bride-to-be would conceive a baby out of wedlock. Despite knowing from prophecy in the scriptures that God would send his saviour to earth through a virgin mother, I very much doubt Joseph hoped God would use 'his' virgin. Despite Joseph's fears and doubts, God saw his faithfulness.

Doubt doesn't mean we have no faith; it means we are uncertain. John the Baptiser, the baby we read about as part of the Christmas story, when in prison as an adult, sent friends to ask Jesus whether he was the Messiah. Jesus didn't criticise his questioning, he simply showed him where to find the answer.

If the opposite of faith is certainty, possibly the very act of wavering shows we are not certain. And if we are not certain but believing somewhat then perhaps that's faith to go on. It takes faith to say to God, 'I don't know how all this is going to work out, and I don't know if I have everything I need to get it done, but if you say so, I'm willing to try.' God meets us in our honest concerns because he knows, without him, we will never have everything we need. It's no surprise to him that we'll need his help.

How easy do you find it to
admit when you waver?

How willing are you to
talk about your doubts
and fears with God?

How kind are you to
yourself when you waver?

Prayer
Father God, there are times when
I waver and get confused about your
purposes. There are times when I doubt your
goodness to me. I know this isn't a surprise to you because
you know me so well and you love me just the same, so
please, in your kindness, draw me closer to you. Amen.

"The Lord has done this for me," she said.
"In these days he has shown his favour and taken
away my disgrace among the people."

LUKE 1: 25

In a loud voice she exclaimed:
"Blessed are you among women, and blessed is the
child you will bear!

LUKE 1: 45

Day 4

A faith expressed

Elizabeth knew that God had achieved for her something that human action could not. When Zechariah returned home following his shift working in the temple, he must somehow communicated to Elizabeth what the angel told him and the two of them slept together. We know so much of Elizabeth and Zechariah's story even down to the praises they both gave to the God they knew deserved the credit for the miracle. For years Elizabeth's personal sadness and social stigma for being unable to conceive and carry a baby must surely have been overwhelming, but once she's sure she's pregnant, she is quick to acknowledge who should be given the credit.

Elizabeth models how we can demonstrate our faith in God through our words and testimony. Elizabeth thanks God for what he had done for her in conceiving a child and credits him with all the glory.

Months later, when Elizabeth greets Mary they share each other's joy and Elizabeth leads them both in acknowledging the wonder of how God is using them both to fulfil his promises to Israel. Both women believe in the Lord and in his promises to them. Elizabeth joyfully acknowledges the sovereignty of the baby Mary is carrying and humbly gives thanks for the honour of meeting her. Ignoring social hierarchy, Elizabeth calls Mary blessed and praises her for her faith in believing God's word.

It is straightforward to see how Elizabeth's pregnancy was a blessing: she was a woman married for a long time to an upright priest, yet was childless. Mary's 'blessing' on the other hand came with the stigma of shame while people gossiped and speculated. What courage it takes to hold on to the faith we know, and to accept that if God has given us something, even if it's painful, it is a blessing and will be used for his glory. Perhaps it's possible that somehow our opinion matters for how much we decide whether something is a blessing in our lives.

Elizabeth's faith in God, trust in her husband and the discernment that came from being filled with the Holy Spirit, convinces Elizabeth of her son's role in the Messiah's plan for the deliverance of Israel. Elizabeth is convinced of his imminent arrival. Elizabeth's firm faith expresses itself over and over again. She shows us, just as she showed Mary, the power of speaking out truth in the faith we know. God knows when we are faithful. He knows when we trust him just as clearly as he knows when we don't.

When Elizabeth gives her son the name John, her friends interrupt 'No one in your family has that name!'[1] and they question her before calling upon Zechariah to settle the matter. Elizabeth's faithful obedience honours God and also honours her husband,

---

1   Luke 1:60

albeit not in the way her neighbours expected.

Elizabeth's repeated expressions of faith in God by carefully attributing his works to him and humbly offering him back all the glory must surely be a valuable model to Mary and a significant witness to her neighbours. Elizabeth will forever know God's power in a personal way and she uses that understanding to point people to the miracle maker.

Declaring aloud where our faith is doesn't boost how God sees us, but it can embolden us and profoundly inspire others. The simple act of expressing our faith to others is a powerful testimony.

Can you think of a time when sharing what God was doing in your life 'ministered' to you as much as the person you were telling?

Have you ever been encouraged by a story of someone else's faith?

Prayer
Thank you for the stories of others that encourage me. Help me see when sharing a story of you working in my life will help someone else. Amen.

In those days Caesar Augustus issued a decree that a census should be taken of the entire Roman world. (This was the first census that took place while Quirinius was governor of Syria.) And everyone went to his own town to register.

So Joseph also went up from the town of Nazareth in Galilee to Judea, to Bethlehem the town of David, because he belonged to the house and line of David. He went there to register with Mary, who was pledged to be married to him and was expecting a child. While they were there, the time came for the baby to be born, and she gave birth to her firstborn, a son. She wrapped him in cloths and placed him in a manger, because there was no room for them in the inn.

LUKE 2: 1-7

"But you, Bethlehem Ephrathah, though you are small among the clans of Judah, out of you will come for me one who will be ruler over Israel, whose origins are from of old, from ancient times."

MICAH 5: 2

Day 5

Interruptions to the faith-filled

Mary stayed with Elizabeth and Zechariah for a few months and then went back to Nazareth to start her life with Joseph. I doubt either of them expected the first months of their marriage would be marked with controversy and, as Joseph had chosen not to consummate their marriage, perhaps a lack of intimacy. As soon as the decree was issued from Caesar Augustus in Rome, rather than settle in to prepare for the approaching arrival of the baby, they were preparing to trek to Bethlehem for the census.

Whether or not we enjoy change or interruption seems to depend on whether we are the ones instigating the interruption or change.

When we feel God asking us to create something or partner with him in a work for his kingdom, we can be inclined to see earthly intrusions as obstructions to be circumnavigated. We can see interruptions to our plans as problems to be solved or bumps to be smoothed out. We may pray that God removes this barrier, or he shows us a way around it.

We do not read of Mary and Joseph trying to find a way around their complication. We don't read of them lamenting that if God really wanted them to have the baby he would find a way to stop their trouble. We don't read of them pleading to be spared the perilous and arduous journey of travelling the 90 miles to Bethlehem.

Looking back, of course, we know that Jesus was supposed to be born in Bethlehem. It wasn't a mistake at all, it was the way it was intended.

As a woman in her third trimester of pregnancy, there's no doubt Mary would have suffered as they walked. (Whether you are a believer in the nativity donkey or not.) Historians calculate Mary and Joseph would likely have walked 10 miles a day, the paths would have been rocky and uneven and the weather at the time incredibly poor. It's exhausting growing a being in your body with or without a maxed-out daily step count and bitter rain. Joseph likely suffered with rising expenses and with what people thought of him, and probably with overwhelming concern for his wife and baby. This world has suffering in it. Sadly, not all God calls us to do is smooth sailing.

Mary & Joseph's faith did not waver despite earthly constraints or decrees, they followed the instructions from Caesar and went to be registered. Perhaps they had the faith to say God's been in it so far and so he will continue to be.

When your life seems a struggle or
you are faced with interruptions,
do you find yourself thinking that
this/that shouldn't be happening?

Do you find yourself wondering 'If this
is God's plan or if God loves me, then
why…'?

What do you think enabled Mary
and Joseph to keep believing God
was in what they were asked to do?

Prayer
God, help me to have patience with
interruptions and look to you to give me what I
need to navigate them. Amen.

For it is by grace you have been saved, through faith—and this is not from yourselves, it is the gift of God— not by works, so that no one can boast.

EPHESIANS 2:8-9

Day 6

Saved through faith by grace

Throughout the whole of our Bible, we can read how God's redemptive plan for his people unfolds. Time and time again we are shown God's love for them by his actions and by his desire they live their best lives. By reading about the tempting of Eve and Adam by the serpent and following the story we understand the need for a saviour and learn about the character of God. We see examples of living according to God's ways and examples of people trying to go it alone. As we look at the whole story we can see and understand the purpose of Jesus' birth, life, death and resurrection and we can give thanks for it.

In the apostle Paul's letter to the Ephesians, we read him reminding the believers that they are saved by grace through faith, not by their works. None of us can assert that anything we've done has in any way contributed to our salvation. The whole thing is a gift from God. The birth of Jesus was the beginning of that gift. His willingness to come to earth and humble himself into a helpless infant marked the start of our redemption story. God's gift of the Holy Spirit to those in Jerusalem following Jesus' ascension to heaven and to the whole world from then on, equips us to grow to be more like Jesus who showed us what perfecting living looked like.

God's people in ancient times lived lives designed to set them apart from the nations around them, their culture distinctive by food laws, dress, societal constructs and their worship rituals. Their scheduled festivals served as intentional reminders of God's character, his mercy, providence and protection. They structured their weeks and their lives around making themselves acceptable to God through the laws they had, but their rituals were never enough to completely atone for their sins and they were never permanent.

> So now there is no condemnation for those who belong to Christ Jesus. And because you belong to him, the power of the life-giving Spirit has freed you from the power of sin that leads to death. The law of Moses was unable to save us because of the weakness of our sinful nature. So God did what the law could not do. He sent his own Son in a body like the bodies we sinners have. And in that body God declared an end to sin's control over us by giving his Son as a sacrifice for our sins. He did this so that the just requirement of the law would be fully satisfied for us, who no longer follow our sinful nature but instead follow the Spirit.
>
> ROMANS 8:1-4 NLT

The result of the Holy Spirit working in our lives includes faithfulness. When we are weak or tired, the power of the Holy Spirit gives us endurance and meets us in our weakness. When faced with a choice to lean into God or to turn away, the Holy Spirit works in us to grow our faithfulness. God's grace made a way for us to be saved from the punishment we deserved, and it makes a way still for us to keep going each day until we get to see him face to face in heaven.

How easy is it to accept salvation
is entirely through God's grace
and all we need to do is believe?

How easy is it for you to accept
that's all that is required for other
people too?

Can you recall a time when the
Holy Spirit in you helped you to
remain faithful to God?

Prayer
God, thank you for your gift of grace
that saved me. Help me to remember this is a
gift available to everyone. Amen.

And you, my child, will be called a prophet of the Most
High; for you will go on before the Lord to prepare
the way for him, to give his people the knowledge of
salvation through the forgiveness of their sins,

LUKE 1: 76-77

Day 7

It's a privilege to be used by God in someone's redemption story

I love what Zechariah sings when his voice is first restored following John's naming. His joy and faith and hope all spill out together. Zechariah praises God for his faithfulness to his people, and for his kindness to redeem them.

While Elizabeth's words recorded earlier in the passage show a woman excited to have a baby and expressing thanks to God with relief as one who has long wished to be a mother. Zechariah makes sure everyone is clear of the reason for his son's appearance: the task and privilege of telling God's people how to know salvation and how to be forgiven of their sins.

And remember, while Zechariah is singing God's praises and celebrating the Messiah, Jesus hasn't yet been born.

As I said before, I like to think Mary was among those present while Zechariah is saying all this. So, if Mary is standing there when everyone gets to hear Zechariah's voice for the first time in almost a year, I wonder whether this was the first time she had heard anyone so joyfully and eloquently define her own purpose in God's plan for the deliverance of Israel. Zechariah, with his status as a temple priest, educated and knowledgeable in Scripture, sings and enthuses about what her baby will become. Sometimes songs and poems can move us more than words in sentences. Mary herself sang when she first arrived with Elizabeth and Zechariah. Perhaps a song allows us to praise in a way that unlocks something in us linked to hope and joy and passion.

Zechariah was thrilled to know that the Messiah was coming, and gladly accepted the role he and Elizabeth had in that story. He was thrilled to be used by God for such a purpose. Just as Elizabeth cried when Mary arrived, 'Why am I so favoured, that the mother of my Lord should come to me?' so Zechariah felt equally honoured to be part of this story. This couple had no doubts about the significance of a deliverer for Israel, nor about his status as God's anointed.

Mary was not coerced by God to carry his son, she committed willingly. The Message translation of her response is 'I am ready to serve.'[1] Her words exquisitely glorifying God and recognising the honour and favour on her show that she saw it a privilege to be part of God's plan for the redemption of his people.

Mary had the faith to believe God had a plan, the faith to believe he would use her specifically, and the faith to keep going even as she endured scorn, shame, and misunderstanding and pain.

When Joseph heard about Mary being pregnant with Jesus, he had a choice to make and he willingly chose to be part of God's plan too. Ultimately, Joseph's faith was in a God who would be on his side, a God who worked on behalf of his people.

---

1   Luke 1:38 MSG

Living in the wilderness and preaching about the Messiah as John the Baptiser did is a very visible work. What we might call A Big Thing. We can often categorise the highly visible kingdom work as more valuable than the stuff fewer people get to see. Growing a baby that would become humanity's saviour like Mary did is A Big Thing. Parenting that Jesus as an infant and toddler and child and teenager is also A Big Thing.

Perhaps we are not called to serve God in such fantastic ways. But who knows how any of the small things we do might affect others in their journey to know God? Serving our family, our neighbours, even strangers, with love and compassion is a way to share our faith. Living and working in the world with the attitude of Christ is the way we show where our faith is. We are not the saviour, but we know who is.

WHO KNOWS HOW ANY OF THE SMALL THINGS WE DO MIGHT AFFECT OTHERS IN THEIR JOURNEY TO KNOW GOD?

Having faith in God who knows all and is above all and submitting to that God can put us in positions to serve that we might never have imagined. Sometimes serving God in a way that completes his plans involves letting go of what we expected our lives to look like. We may need to humble ourselves or let go of something we saw as important in order to be used as God desires in someone else's story.

God might call each of us to serve in endlessly different ways, but it is always our honour to be used by him. It a privilege to be used in any way that contributes to someone else's redemption story.

Do you think serving others
can be a way to serve God?

Do you think we all have
chances to be part of God's
plans to reach other people?

Do you agree that even the smallest
things we do can affect others and how
they see God, even to how they might
come to know God for themselves?

Have you ever had to let go of something you thought was important in order to be obedient to God or serve his purposes in some way?

Prayer
God, its amazing that you desire us to work with you to accomplish your plans on earth.
Show me ways I can serve others so they can have their own redemption story. Amen.

If this is all you have time for this week...

If hope is looking forward to something, perhaps faith is the belief that it's possible.

FAITH IN A DEPENDABLE GOD While the earthly things in which we put our faith can turn out to be inadequate, faith in God is solid because he is dependable. God is infinite and unchanging, all-knowing, all-powerful and present everywhere at once. Our faith isn't in God doing things the way we think he should, or in our circumstances turning out the way we imagine they will: faith in God is believing he is who he says he is.

FAITH IS A CHOICE, AND A CONTINUAL CHOICE The Christmas story has multiple characters who each had to make a choice between having faith in what they saw or heard in the earthly world or having faith in the God they knew. Having questions about God, wondering if we are making the correct choices, coming back to God and pondering are *not* markers of faithlessness. God, who is not intimidated by anything we might think or do, meets us in our questions. Faith is our choice to believe that God is good, that he wants us to draw close to him, and that he made a way to save us. We may have puzzling questions or stumble on our way sometimes but these on their own do not mean we don't have faith.

FOCUS ON THE PROVIDER Faith is focussing on the provider rather than how we think our need will best be met. Faith is focussing on the one who heals rather than the process by which we think our body or mind will be cured. Faith is focussing on the ultimate relationship restorer rather than making plans of how we think our lives should look.

Speaking out about the faithful God we know, sharing our questions openly, praising God for the bits we do understand and watching for how God meets us, all sustain our faith and help us persevere while we walk out our lives. Sharing those things out loud can also help strengthen and encourage others.

THE CHRISTMAS STORY PEOPLE ARE REAL PEOPLE TOO The names of those in the Christmas story can seem familiar to us who've been to church or who grew up with the nativity as part of our holiday festivities, but we do well to remember that these characters were real people before they became characters. When we read their stories, we see each of them considered it a privilege to be used by God in some way to forward his plan for the redemption of humankind. We remember the story of Jesus' birth and put it in the context of his whole life. By putting our faith in Jesus and acknowledging his work on earth, we are saved and called children of God.

THINGS WE DO CAN CHANGE LIVES At Christmas, we recall those who stepped out in faith to be part of the story of God's redemption for his people. Whether their role was big or small, whether the role looked like a blessing or came with personal costs, each of them served willingly knowing that God's plans were transformational. When we are willing, we too can be used by God in his plans to draw others near to him. Even the unseen or the small things can make a difference. Forgiving someone, being patient with someone, serving someone, putting someone else's needs above our own might seem unremarkable but could play a huge role in someone coming to know God.

It's a privilege to be used by God in someone's redemption story

joy

The people walking in darkness have seen a great light; on those living in the land of deep darkness a light has dawned. You have enlarged the nation and increased their joy; they rejoice before you as people rejoice at the harvest, as warriors rejoice when dividing the plunder.

ISAIAH 9:2-4

Day 1

What is joy?

The word joy seems to be used a lot more at Christmastime than the rest of the year. I don't think I've ever asked my kids, 'Did you have joy at football today?' I think joy can seem like an old-fashioned word, a word we reserve for 'special' occasions.

In this passage from Isaiah, the word we see translated as joy is the ancient Hebrew word *simchah* and can be described also as mirth or gladness. (Neither of those are words are in my everyday vocabulary, either.) To help us understand its meaning better, we can look where else it's used in the Bible and, doing that, we find it's used to describe happiness and relief, for example when towns-people celebrated once the men arrived back home safe and victorious from battle. Happiness and relief are words I do use in my everyday.

Today's verse from Isaiah's prophecy speaks of a time to come when the Israelites are delivered by the Messiah and they react with gladness. The prophet highlights experiences they can think of (bountiful harvest, sharing out treasure) to help them imagine their future rejoicing then. The simplest definition of joy how we tend to use it might just be 'the emotion of great delight or happiness caused by something exceptionally good' because typically we associate joy with the exceptional rather than the everyday. When we looking at the moments of expressed joy in the Christmas story this definition seems to fit well.

Who doesn't show happiness (joy) to some extent when good things occur?

Have you ever watched a film that thrilled you and then gone on to recommend the watching of it to a friend or colleague? Or perhaps you've enthused to neighbour about a new coffee place you found? Or posted on social media about a cake or dessert or meal you ate? Or shared with everyone a fitness regime that's improved your wellbeing? Who doesn't share good personal news with their friends, like when we find a new job after a period of waiting for one, or when we receive medical test results telling us we are healthy? When we feel joy over something, we can't help but enthuse about it. Somehow telling others of our enjoyment adds to our happiness, or we might call it joy.

TELLING OTHERS ABOUT OF OUR ENJOYMENT SEEMS TO ADD TO OUR OWN HAPPINESS

C. S. Lewis in his book *Reflection On The Psalms* wrote that 'enjoyment spontaneously overflows into praise' until some other emotion or action stops it. We can't help but praise (tell about it) when we find something enjoyable. Praise is our expression of enjoyment. In the same book, Lewis also wrote the praise we give 'not merely expresses but completes the enjoyment.' Imagine: joy continues unbounded until something else causes it to stop and joy is not complete until it is expressed somehow.

The trouble with reserving the word joy only for the can't-stop-talking, hand-clapping, jumping-up-and-down thing we see in cartoons is that we miss out on noticing it at other times. What about the quiet joy of a grandparent seeing an infant of a new generation playing on a carpet or learning to walk? Or the speechless joy of someone who gets a good medical test result after a long time of gruelling treatment? What about the proverbial tears of joy?

If we only consider joy as one extreme end of a spectrum of enjoyment, how do we explain when we feel joy alongside other emotions? The third day after Jesus was crucified, some women went to the tomb to start preparing his buried body and, unexpectedly to them, Jesus met them, fully alive. The scriptures say the women 'hurried away from the tomb, afraid yet filled with joy, and ran to tell his disciples.'[1] These women had the joy of seeing their friend alive again, but were said to also be afraid. We don't read of them stopping to dance, sing or clap their hands.

In the Bible in the book of Galatians[2], we are given a list of indicators that the Holy Spirit working in us: love, joy, peace, patience, goodness, gentleness, kindness, faithfulness and self-control. If this list would only refer to feelings, then these characteristics have the potential to show up sometimes but not others.

1   Matthew 28:8
2   Galatians 5

If instead, we consider these nine things as a set of behaviours, it's easier to grasp how they can coexist. The Holy Spirit is plainly working in us when we feel confused but still demonstrate patience, kindness and joy; when we feel afraid but still react with love, self-control and joy.

Do you only use the word joy
to describe a perfect kind of
enjoyment, that is, do you reserve
the word joy for 'special occasions'?

Has anyone or anything made you
feel you need to stop feelings of
happiness or joy, or perhaps not
express them?

Do you agree that joy can
be a behaviour or lifestyle?

How do you feel about joy
being able to coexist with
other feelings?

Prayer
Thank you for joy, for happiness, and the
things that bring us those emotions. Help us to
embrace them and be grateful for them. Amen.

At that time Mary got ready and hurried to a town in the hill country of Judea, where she entered Zechariah's home and greeted Elizabeth. When Elizabeth heard Mary's greeting, the baby leaped in her womb, and Elizabeth was filled with the Holy Spirit. In a loud voice she exclaimed: "Blessed are you among women, and blessed is the child you will bear! But why am I so favoured, that the mother of my Lord should come to me? As soon as the sound of your greeting reached my ears, the baby in my womb leaped for joy. Blessed is she who has believed that the Lord would fulfil his promises to her!"

And Mary said: "My soul glorifies the Lord and my spirit rejoices in God my Saviour, for he has been mindful of the humble state of his servant. From now on all generations will call me blessed, for the Mighty One has done great things for me—holy is his name. His mercy extends to those who fear him, from generation to generation. He has performed mighty deeds with his arm; he has scattered those who are proud in their inmost thoughts. He has brought down rulers from their thrones but has lifted up the humble. He has filled the hungry with good things but has sent the rich away empty. He has helped his servant Israel, remembering to be merciful to Abraham and his descendants forever, just as he promised our ancestors.

LUKE 1:39-45

Day 2

The gift of joy

Luke's gospel tells us that one of the first things Mary did after hearing from the angel Gabriel was to visit her relative Elizabeth who was also unexpectedly carrying a child. We're told that when Elizabeth heard Mary's voice the baby (who would grow up to be called John the Baptiser) leapt for joy in her womb. Whether Elizabeth had already heard Mary's news or whether she was divinely informed, I don't know, but she knows she is greeting the mother of her Lord.

The baby in her womb is moved, Elizabeth is moved, and she expresses her delight with praise. Elizabeth praises God as she understands what's happening at last: the long-awaited Messiah is on the way.

Perhaps Mary felt nervous coming up to Zechariah and Elizabeth's home. Perhaps she felt trepidation walking through their village. Perhaps she'd heard whispers from the folk she passed as she travelled. With no instant messaging platforms, Mary would have no clues regarding Elizabeth's reaction until she saw it in real life.

What a relief it must have been. To be greeted with such joy and to know straightaway she was believed must have been such an encouragement to her spirit. Surely, it's no coincidence that right after this greeting, Mary's own song of praise is recorded. Mary sings of the powerful acts God's performed for his people and appreciates his heart towards his people

> FEW THINGS INSPIRE CREATIVITY AND KINDLE JOY MORE THAN SOMEONE TRULY STANDING WITH US AND CHEERING US ON

Nothing kills excitement or pleasure more than someone whose opinion we care about reacting negatively. And few things inspire creativity and kindle joy more than someone truly standing with us and cheering us on.

Mary's decision to visit Elizabeth may have come from necessity following the news about her conception, or it may have been Mary's own desire to spend time with someone who was also experiencing a miracle pregnancy. The angel Gabriel told Mary about Elizabeth's pregnancy as proof that nothing was impossible for God. We can assume that Mary must have known Zechariah and Elizabeth were unable to have children, and so to see Elizabeth six months pregnant at her advanced age would be evidence of divine and miraculous intervention. So often, seeing how God has worked in the lives of others helps us accept he can also work in our own lives.

How far do other people's
reactions to your thoughts, ideas
or plans (whether divinely sent
or otherwise) affect how you feel
about them?

Have you ever had the
opportunity to respond
with joy to something and
instead reacted negatively?

Do you agree that seeing
someone else's joy can
sometimes give us permission
to express our own?

Prayer
Help us to respond to others with
encouragement and joy. Help us to see the joy
Jesus brings. Amen.

His father Zechariah was filled with the Holy Spirit and prophesied: "Praise be to the Lord, the God of Israel, because he has come to his people and redeemed them. He has raised up a strong king of salvation for us in the house of his servant David (as he said through his holy prophets of long ago), salvation from our enemies and from the hand of all who hate us—to show mercy to our ancestors and to remember his holy covenant, the oath he swore to our father Abraham: to rescue us from the hand of our enemies, and to enable us to serve him without fear in holiness and righteousness before him all our days. And you, my child, will be called a prophet of the Most High; for you will go on before the Lord to prepare the way for him, to give his people the knowledge of salvation through the forgiveness of their sins, because of the tender mercy of our God, by which the rising sun will come to us from heaven to shine on those living in darkness and in the shadow of death, to guide our feet into the path of peace."

LUKE 1:67-79

Day 3

Revealing joy

As a consequence of questioning the reliability of the angel Gabriel's message to him about him and his wife becoming parents at their advanced age, Zechariah was rendered mute. While his inability to speak was a demonstrable sign to everyone of his encounter in the temple, so also must his voice's sudden return have been ten months later at his son's naming ceremony.

After being mute for almost a year Zechariah uses his first words to sing in praise to God and prophesy of the future. Perhaps his muteness made him realise what a privilege a voice was. Perhaps after his long-enforced silence he is now fundamentally certain who has the authority. The first use of his voice directs all his listeners to God. He doesn't make it about himself. He doesn't start with 'Let me tell you what happened to me that day in the temple…' Zechariah goes straight to, 'Let me tell you about my God.' We can be reasonably confident that the people around him, his friends and family and neighbours, all knew God, but that doesn't mean Zechariah allows them to come to their own conclusions. He takes the initiative. He summarises what he's learned about God through the recent season of miracles and powerfully reminds everyone of God's character and his plan for their ultimate redemption.

Zechariah's song gives joyful praise to the God he's known all his life but who has recently demonstrated his almighty power personally and he asserts key things he's learned about God during his lifetime: God's nearness, God's power, God's promise of redemption, and God's mercy, faithfulness, gentleness and kindness.

While Zechariah's words declare his own joy and delight, they also give language to the joy that should be expressed by the whole world.

ZECHARIAH'S WORDS GIVE LANGUAGE TO THE JOY THAT SHOULD BE EXPRESSED BY THE WHOLE WORLD

As Zechariah moves on to prophesy over his son and his son's calling, he affirms all the angel Gabriel told him in the temple about his son's ministry. As a priest in the temple himself, Zechariah understands the need for his son to prepare God's people for the Messiah. Zechariah firmly attributes all the saving power and all the forgiveness of sins to the coming Messiah with immense and clear joy. Such exuberance before John can walk and before Jesus has even been born! It would be understandable if he waited to praise God until John was past infancy, or until he could see evidence John was a man of godly character, but he doesn't wait. If Zechariah is tempted to imagine all the possible ways things could go wrong, he doesn't show it, praise flows immediately and fluently. He has learnt not to need to see evidence to be sure but to act in the firm belief that nothing is impossible for God.

Praising God for things he hasn't done yet takes faith. There's a boldness that accompanies the willingness to say out loud and publicly, 'This is what I believe God is going to do.' There's a confidence that's required when we do what's not expected of us. Zechariah's joy in what God can and will do is impressive. Whether at the naming ceremony or at any other time, I am guessing that Zechariah's joy was evident to everyone. He takes no credit for John's birth or John's commission. What a blessing for Elizabeth to see her husband praising God for their shared miracle.

Do you feel that you have things
you can be joyful about?

Has there ever been a time when
you felt it would be too much of a
risk to express joy?

Prayer
Father God, fill us with joy and give us ways to
express it. Amen.

And there were shepherds living out in the fields nearby, keeping watch over their flocks at night. An angel of the Lord appeared to them, and the glory of the Lord shone around them, and they were terrified.

But the angel said to them, "Do not be afraid. I bring you good news that will cause great joy for all the people. Today in the town of David a Saviour has been born to you; he is the Messiah, the Lord. This will be a sign to you: You will find a baby wrapped in cloths and lying in a manger."

Suddenly a great company of the heavenly host appeared with the angel, praising God and saying, "Glory to God in the highest heaven, and on earth peace to those on whom his favour rests."

LUKE 2:8-14

Day 4

Joy isn't only an earthly thing

For the shepherds, after hundreds of years of silence from God, there is no denying this heavenly announcement. The whole group of them at once saw a spectacle of light and glory and singing. To prevent panic, the angels famously tell the shepherds that the news they bring is good news and it will cause great joy for all people.

And the angels know just how good this news is.

Angels who have been present from when God created the world, who are witnesses to all that has happened since and who are commissioned by God as messengers would naturally be most able to appreciate the joy surrounding the birth of Jesus. Since the fall, when sin entered the world, they have anticipated this moment knowing it would be the beginning of Christ's work on earth. Jesus Christ wasn't created when he was born on earth, the angels would have known him all along, but they were positioned to appreciate that his descent to earth was the start of salvation for humankind. Despite the fact they knew they would have to wait for him to be weaned and to grow to adulthood, their delight in his manifestation couldn't help but be broadcast. Their joy bursts out.

Don't we also celebrate when we see progress?

Don't we celebrate milestones and accomplished goals?

For most of us, our good news affects only those immediately around us. But this event, this special birth affected the whole of humanity at the time and forever. No wonder the angels were so able to declare that the news would bring joy for all people. They tell the shepherds where to find the baby and what to expect, assuming quite rightly the shepherds would want to see for themselves.

During his earthly ministry, Jesus tells some parables to people around him to show how wonderful it is to be reconciled to God when we feel lost or left behind. The stories he tells are to show his listeners how God doesn't give up on us when we go astray and, in fact, he searches for us. Jesus talks of a shepherd who searches for a lost sheep, a woman who searches for a valuable coin she lost, and a father who eagerly waits for his wayward son to return. We can hear those stories and take from them how much we are loved by God and how he desires us to come to him, no matter how far we stray. But Jesus also talks about the joy of those who find the things they lost. Both the shepherd, the woman, and the father in the stories invite their neighbours to join

GOD DOESN'T GIVE UP ON US WHEN WE GO ASTRAY, IN FACT, HE SEARCHES FOR US

in and celebrate. Additionally, we learn earthly creatures are not the only ones to experience joy.

Jesus says tells his listeners that just like those characters in the stories who rejoice when their lost things are found, so there is rejoicing in heaven—the very angels in God's presence are joyful—when even one sinner repents and turns to God.

What a surprising and delightful picture for us to imagine. When we take paths that lead us to dark places we can at times feel embarrassed as if we are the only ones to ever take a wrong turn or walk away from the best place to be. Sometimes our shame at the realisation of where we got to, inadvertently or otherwise, can make it harder to come back to where we know we would be better off. Our feelings of disgrace can keep us trapped and compound our misery. We can believe we are 'a lost cause' and sadness or the consequences of our actions are all we deserve. If we do start to consider we could return, sometimes we might feel we must clean ourselves up a bit before we can be presentable enough to start walking home. As Jesus speaks to those gathered around him he tells only heaven's over our return. There is no mention of the wrongs we have done, no mention of anything we need to do except believe we can come. No mention of clearing up our mess first, only of our turning to repent. What joy and relief this can bring us if we accept it.

Just as the angels came to earth to announce and celebrate Jesus' birth, there is rejoicing in heaven over our re-birth when we come to Jesus personally as our saviour. This knowledge should spur us on to tell our story of redemption to others who haven't heard. Our stories can lead others to the hope and freedom available through Jesus and give heaven more reasons to celebrate.

Have you ever imagined angels in heaven rejoicing over you?

Do you have friends or family that haven't accepted the forgiveness available to them through Jesus?

Have you ever thought you must
clean yourself up a bit before you
can come to God?

Do you think your story of how
you found forgiveness in Jesus
might encourage someone you
know to consider Jesus would
welcome them also?

What would you say to someone
who said, 'Jesus wouldn't want
someone like me'?

Prayer
God, It's incredible to think that the
angels in heaven rejoice whenever
someone turns to you and accepts
forgiveness. Help us remember there is
nothing that can separate us from your love
and nothing is too bad for you to forgive. Amen.

You make known to me the path of life; in your presence there is fullness of joy; at your right hand are pleasures forevermore.

PSALM 16:11 ESV

Though you have not seen him, you love him; and even though you do not see him now, you believe in him and are filled with an inexpressible and glorious joy, for you are receiving the end result of your faith, the salvation of your souls.

1 PETER 1:8

Day 5

Joy for a reason

When we imagine a joyful person, I think we can often think of only something like a certain animated princess. This person glides through life with a perpetual smile, graceful patience and an abundance of friendly woodland creatures skipping along beside her, even as she chokes on a poisoned apple and drops down as if dead. I don't think we usually imagine them as people who look exactly like us.

The feelings we experience in our lives on earth are temporary, changeable and dependent on our circumstances. We feel sad after watching a poignant story in an advertisement or movie; we feel anger when we are denied something we feel we needed; we feel pleasure when we get something we want; we feel jealous when a colleague gets the promotion we feel we deserved. Yet, all these feelings are temporary and we may experience many, many different feelings in the course of the day.

Unlike the transitory feelings we experience on earth, the joy we feel in God's presence in heaven will be complete and eternal.

Crucifixion is agonizingly painful and would never be likely discussed with joy, and yet we are told that Jesus endured the manner of his death for the 'joy set before him.' [Hebrews 12:2b] What was the joy set before him? The joy was knowing our salvation would be assured and we would be reconciled with God. His obedience to the purpose given to him by his father and the knowledge that we would be admitted to heaven was the joy that enabled him to endure his torturous death.

We can express our joy at Mary's pregnancy and Jesus' birth in Bethlehem because those actions set in motion the means of our salvation. The fact we live after Jesus' birth, death and resurrection means we don't have to live with the fear that God won't be with us, or that he won't hear us when we pray. By living where we are in history, we can know we are never separated from God's love and that we are now in no way condemned. We can be free from

WE CAN KNOW WE ARE NEVER SEPARATED FROM GOD'S LOVE AND THAT WE ARE NOW IN NO WAY CONDEMNED

any worries regarding being accepted by God and are free to be able to say joyfully, 'I am forgiven. I don't fear punishment. I am free from the shame of my less than perfect behaviour.'

The way our joy tends to visibly manifest depends on our own individual character personalities. I've seen people dance and jump around in church as they try to express their joy over their forgiven lives. I've seen others sit with tears rolling down their faces, while others sit still and quiet almost in meditation. In the accounts of Jesus' life on earth, we can see he experiences every emotion we do, yet I can't find any reference to him jumping or dancing with joy. Perhaps joy is not connected to cardio-activity.

What we do see in the scriptures showing Jesus' joy is him expressing thanks and praise to his father. One day when Jesus the disciplines come back revelling in their accomplishments, he reminds them to focus on what is truly cause for celebration: their names were written in heaven. Jesus points quite clearly at the bigger reason to celebrate and then shows them how. We read that Jesus 'full of joy by the Holy Spirit' started straight-away praising his father. The appropriate display of our joy and celebration for our salvation is thanks and praise to God. The joy in Jesus expressed itself in praise to his father from where everything comes. Perhaps joy is less about leaping around and more about knowing where to focus.

We were not present at Jesus' birth, nor with him during his earthly ministry and yet we can rejoice in all that we have due to him:

- Assurance of a place in heaven

- Direct access to God through prayer

- Restoration of our relationship with our father God as children

- Elimination of the punishments that our sin deserved

- Constantly accompanied and never abandoned

When we choose to call to mind that Jesus is our saviour, think about the impact of that in our lives today and for our eternal future, we should express that delight to the one who made the redemption plan in the first place. And Jesus showed us exactly how.

How do you show joy?

How often do you think
of your salvation through
Christ as something to be
joyful about?

Have you ever been
confused by someone
else's different way of
expressing joy?

Do you think Christians
are typically characterised
by their joyfulness?

Prayer
God, help us to remember there is
joy in our salvation and being joyful is   an
appropriate response. Amen.

Now there was a man in Jerusalem called Simeon, who was righteous and devout. He was waiting for the consolation of Israel, and the Holy Spirit was on him. It had been revealed to him by the Holy Spirit that he would not die before he had seen the Lord's Messiah.

Moved by the Spirit, he went into the temple courts. When the parents brought in the child Jesus to do for him what the custom of the Law required, Simeon took him in his arms and praised God, saying: "Sovereign Lord, as you have promised, you may now dismiss your servant in peace. For my eyes have seen your salvation, which you have prepared in the sight of all nations: a light for revelation to the Gentiles, and the glory of your people Israel."

LUKE 2:25-32

Day 6

Willing to see

Some days after Jesus' birth someone else gets to experience the joy of realising the journey to humanity's salvation has at last begun. Jesus is taken by his parents to the temple so they can offer the customary sacrifices for a first-born son. Simeon, a devout man who worshipped God, recognises Jesus for who is and comes straight over to meet the family. His hope for Israel's deliverance and his joy at seeing it manifest overflows to praise. Simeon praised God for what was beginning even though, due to his age, he was unlikely to live to see the rescue of his people.

Perhaps Simeon's joy came from realising the Holy Spirit's promise to him personally had been fulfilled (we read earlier in the passage that he had been told by the Holy Spirit that he wouldn't die until he'd seen the Messiah). Perhaps he was simply overjoyed to confirm without a doubt, like Zechariah, Mary and Elizabeth before him, that God is faithful. Hope and peace were coming.

It takes hope and faith to keep believing when you feel time is running out. As Simeon got older and older and had not seen an anointed deliverer for Israel he may have been tempted to give up or to consider he had misunderstood. Even at this point, he could have experienced bitterness from realising things hadn't worked out how he expected them to, he would not get to actually see Israel's deliverance.

Everyone else in the temple, at best, saw only a poor couple preparing to complete a temple ritual but Simeon saw God's redemptive plan. Simeon's spirit-filled watchfulness allowed him to see what others didn't. Simeon's lifelong faithfulness enabled his outpouring of joyful expression. What a privilege and reward for him!

SIMEON'S SPIRIT-FILLED WATCHFULNESS ALLOWED HIM TO SEE WHAT OTHERS DIDN'T

When the shepherds are visited by the angel and told that the Messiah was born in the nearby town, they had a choice whether to find him or not. The reward of seeking the Messiah was shared joy and wonder with Mary and Joseph and then later, shared wonder with everyone they told. Luke 2:18 tells us that all who heard were amazed and marvelled.

The coming of Jesus was truly marvellous in more ways than they were yet to fully appreciate, but they could have easily missed out on the joy had they not gone to see.

What might we miss out on
because we're not open to what
the spirit wants to show us?

Have you ever allowed your joy
to be overshadowed because
things didn't work out the way
you'd imagined?

Prayer
Father God, Open our eyes so may we
not miss out on what your spirit wants to show
us. Amen.

When it was time for Elizabeth to have her baby, she gave birth to a son. Her neighbours and relatives heard that the Lord had shown her great mercy, and they shared her joy.

LUKE 1:57-58

Day 7

It's a privilege to share in one-another's joy

The angel who visited Zechariah told him his son would be a 'joy and delight' to him. For Elizabeth and Zechariah who had desperately hoped for a child for so many years, I think that might be obvious. But the angel also said, 'many will rejoice because of his birth.' Not just Elizabeth and Zechariah would rejoice, but many.

When we watch a friend hope and wait for something for a long time it is usual to express joy when we see their dream finally come true. It's good to share in one another's joy. A college acceptance, a new job, a pay-rise, a marriage proposal, a new baby, all these things can bring us joy when they happen to us but also cause us joy when they happen to those we love. It doesn't take a great deal of imagination to think that many of Elizabeth's friends would be thrilled she was having a baby after so many years of hoping.

It's a privilege to have relationships that mean when good things happen we are just as pleased for our friends as we would be for ourselves. I would assume Elizabeth was not the only woman in Judea to ever struggle to conceive then reach an age where everyone would think her chance of motherhood was over. Elizabeth wasn't always old, and I imagine some younger women also hoped for babies but had not yet conceived. Other women who also experienced infertility could choose whether to be happy that Elizabeth has this blessing or be bitter that they had not. In one scenario they are choosing to share in their friend's joy, in the other choosing to focus on their own lack. If we let it, joining in other's joy can create something like joy in us. If we allow it, celebrating someone's provision reminds us that good things can also happen to us. If God heals or provides for our friend we are reassured that God still works on our behalf.

If expressing our own enjoyment somehow completes it, feasibly sharing in someone else's joy can multiply it. Sharing in the joy of others is a privilege because it shows we have people in our lives, relationships of value to us, even when we might feel we have nothing to celebrate.

When Paul writes to the believers in Rome to outline the kind of behaviours that show

WHEN OUR FRIENDS OR NEIGHBOURS ARE CELEBRATING, LOVING THEM WELL MEANS SHARING THEIR JOY TOO

Christ-like love in action, one thing he commands is rejoicing with those who rejoice.[1] When our friends or neighbours are celebrating, loving them well means sharing their joy too. What kind of friend would not?

---

1   Romans 12:15

When Mary was visited by the shepherds I would imagine she would have seen joy in their faces. Still exhilarated from a vision of heavenly beings lighting up their night sky but perhaps a little apprehensive, they enter a small room where there really was a baby, just like the angels described. Then the realisation: if part of the angel's message was true then all of it was true. This is the Messiah! Their curiosity must surely have turned to joy.

These shepherds, who some think might have been the men and women who raised lambs for the temple sacrifices, would surely have shared how they came to hear about Jesus. In sharing their story, surely Mary's own heart was nourished as she recalled once more the angel Gabriel's words from nine months earlier. This son would be the Messiah. These shepherds might have asked, 'Is it true? Is this baby the Messiah?' and she might have answered, 'Well, that's what the angel who visited me said.' And they gazed at the baby in his makeshift crib and imagined ahead to a time when he would deliver them from the oppression they had grown tired of.

In Mary's exhaustion from travel and giving birth, perhaps the shepherd's joy kindled her own. Her baby who likely looked like most other babies was none the less unique: an angel had told her, an angel had told Joseph, and now more angels had told these shepherds. The shepherd's visit and the joy they demonstrated would surely have been a great gift to her.

Whether we are sharing in the joy coming from the news of a friend's good fortune, or the outcome of a team project in our community, or the testimony of someone telling of their salvation, it is a privilege to be trusted to share in their joy.

Can you think of a time when sharing in someone else's joy made you feel happy yourself?

How easy is it to see people we don't like experience joy?

Do you think it's possible to
be moved by something joyful
happening to a stranger? Or
only those we love?

Prayer
Holy Spirit, Show us ways we can love those
around us by sharing joy. Reveal to us those who
need someone to celebrate with. Amen.

If this is all you have time for this week...

JOY ISN'T A WORD WE USE A LOT While joy may feel like a big, old-fashioned word that gets only used for church and Christmas, it's an appropriately rich word to use when we consider the full purpose of Jesus' birth and its enormous benefit to us.

JOY FOR ALL The angels who announced Jesus' birth were joyful and told the shepherds that the birth would bring joy to everyone. God, from his great love and in his faithfulness to us, sent his son to show us the way to be reconciled to him. The shepherds didn't realise this yet, but standing here in the 21st century we can understand far more. The birth of this baby set into tangible motion the events that would lead to our permanent forgiveness. That's the good news.

FORGIVENESS IS CAUSE FOR JOY When Jesus' grew up he spent three years preaching and teaching those who would listen what a relationship with God looked like. Following his death, resurrection and ascension to heaven, his followers continued to tell as many as they could, spreading out through the regions. They shared the message with those they met with joy and enthusiasm because they wanted everyone to share in it. It wasn't a message they wanted to keep to themselves: it was too good not to share.

JOY IN HEAVEN Whenever someone on earth makes a decision to accept the good news of forgiveness through Jesus, the whole of heaven rejoices. A reason the angels were so able to declare to the shepherds that Jesus' birth was good news for everyone was because they get to see first hand the party of gladness in heaven when we turn to Jesus. If you have chosen to accept the forgiveness Jesus offers, the angels rejoiced over you. They rejoice every time.

JOY IS OUR STRENGTH When we choose to accept the free gift from God that Jesus made possible for us, we can build our lives on a foundation of lasting joy that enables us to endure all manner of other circumstances and feelings. This world as we know it and the circumstances we experience are not the end; we have a future in heaven where all our troubles will be gone. While we experience trouble in our earthly lifetime, we have a friend in Jesus who equips us to keep going and to live in love. Of course, we do also experience good things while we live on earth. When we look for them, we can notice the joy and the causes of joy all around us.

SHARING MULTIPLIES JOY During our lives on earth we build relationships with school friends and neighbours and work colleagues and friends and friends of friends. Each of those relationships provides opportunities to not only share our joy but to share in theirs. When we share our joy with someone else somehow we are also uplifted. When we share in another person's joy somehow become joy-filled too.

There are so many ways that sharing joy in our friendship circles and neighbourhoods and communities brings us together.

It's a privilege to share in one-another's joy

Peace

I have told you these things, so that in me you may
have peace. In this world you will have trouble. But
take heart! I have overcome the world.

JOHN 16:33

Day 1

What is peace?

The concept of peace is so universal in so many cultures that most languages have a word for it simple enough to be in everyone's vocabulary. A least at first, we might most often consider peace to be synonymous with quiet, or perhaps, simply the opposite of conflict or war.

The word translated peace in the Old Testament is *shalom*. Interestingly, if you were to look it up in a dictionary of ancient Hebrew the first few meanings listed would be to do with completeness, safety and wholeness. In the story of Joseph (not Mary's husband but the one with a fancy colourful coat who was sold into Ancient Egyptian slavery), the word *shalom* is used by his brothers when they tell him their father is well and in good health. To those Hebrew speaking people, the word *shalom* meant more than what we think of when we speak of peace: the word had connotations of bringing things to order, or back to wholeness as if restoring something.

In Mark's gospel, we read of a woman who, suffering from constant bleeding for twelve years, surreptitiously and silently reaches out to Jesus in the hope the touch in itself will bring healing. When Jesus becomes aware of this action he stops walking and calls out to the person who touched him. As the trembling woman reveals herself, Jesus says, 'Your faith has healed you. Go in peace and be freed from your suffering.'[1] The command that she go 'in peace' is more than a reference to her nervousness or fear, or even at her exhilaration at being healed, it points to the fact that she is now restored to wholeness. The woman is no longer separated from society due to her condition and she no longer needs to live in pain: she is completely restored.

Many of the laws we read in the early books of the Old Testament relate to restitution of property following loss or damage by someone: the Israelites were told how to broker peace by reimbursement and by making amends. The Biblical way of looking at peace is not simply that we don't fight anymore, but that we make restitution and we work together. In English when we say two teams are working peaceably with each other we don't merely mean they aren't being combative; we mean they are being collaborative. When we imagine two people are working peaceably together, they might be sharing tools or materials or helping each other in some way.

The majority of us do not face the fear and insecurity of war nor do we face the day to day realities of violent conflict. For most of us reading this, when we hope for peace in our own lives, we are probably thinking more

1   Mark 5:34

of rest rather than relief from immediate danger. We call things peaceful when there is little manufactured noise, perhaps when we hear only the sounds of nature, or the crackling of logs on a fire, or the gentle snores of a favourite pet.

Not long before he was taken to be crucified Jesus is recorded talking to the disciples, predicting his death and talking about the coming of the Holy Spirit. He anticipates their grief while explaining how all this is ultimately for their good. He concludes this somewhat confusing and gloomy conversation by saying, 'I have told you these things, so that in me you may have peace. In this world you will have trouble. But take heart! I have overcome the world.'[2] Using the word peace in this context he can hardly be talking about quietness, rest or tranquillity. How can they experience quiet when hundreds will be chanting for their friend's death? How can they possibly feel calm while their friend is being treated unjustly? Once Jesus ascends to heaven and his followers tell everyone about Jesus' life and purpose they will experience discrimination and suffering, in some cases to the point of torture and death. How could they experience peace under those circumstances? How could anyone?

Perhaps we must consider that when Jesus talks of peace he isn't talking about the absence-from-worldly-conflict kind of peace but something bigger and wider than we can easily imagine. Jesus lived subject to complications from a governance structure imposed

---

2   John 16:33

by Roman rule. Jesus also experienced the conflict that comes from being at odds with family as even his own brothers hated him during his ministry.

Jesus was the path of peace, he acted peacefully and he urged his disciples when the sent them out to go in peace. And yet, living as a Christ-follower can bring dissension.

When we declare our allegiance to Jesus we can open ourselves up to criticism and misunderstanding from those who do not consider Jesus the Lord. When we choose a lifestyle that resembles the one Jesus modelled, we can automatically make ourselves look distinct from those around us and that difference can bring disagreement. Declaring and demonstrating the peace with have with God through Jesus Christ can bring discord with those around us. All of these things can feel like the opposite of our simplest, everyday definition of peace.

Believing and remembering that Jesus has overcome the world when the world seems against us can feel impossible unless we expand our view of what peace is. Yet our own definition of peace can define how we act.

What things do you
associate with peace?

How does the concept of
peace as wholeness or safety or
completeness resonate with you?

Does considering peace as 'being
restored' or 'being made whole
again' change how you think
about the message the angels
brought to the shepherds?

Have you ever experienced conflict or
unexpected detachment with someone
because of your faith in Jesus?

Prayer
Thank you, Jesus, for your
tremendous sacrifice in coming
to earth as fully human, and as a
completely dependent baby, in order
that we might know and understand
and receive the peace with God that only your
work could do. Amen.

For to us a child is born, to us a son is given, and the government will be on his shoulders. And he will be called Wonderful Counsellor, Mighty God, Everlasting Father, Prince of Peace. Of the greatness of his government and peace there will be no end. He will reign on David's throne and over his kingdom, establishing and upholding it with justice and righteousness from that time on and forever. The zeal of the Lord Almighty will accomplish this.

ISAIAH 9:6-7

Day 2

Prince of Peace

Hundreds of years before Mary and Joseph headed to Bethlehem to take part in Caesar's census, the prophet Isaiah wrote about a future king of Israel. Isaiah lists the attributes this future king will have and also the outcome of his reign. Because of this prophecy, the nation of Israel looked forward to a king who would bring peace to their land, eradicating occupation and oversight from any foreign power. Isaiah calls him 'Prince of Peace' and goes on to say the peace he brings will never end. To a nation at the mercy of foreign rule and who lived with very real threats of oppression, this must have been quite something to look forward to.

As the years went by and any personal memories of being a feared nation faded, the thought that a warrior like their beloved King David would come and overthrow their illegitimate rulers must have been an amazing hope. Once their enemies were defeated and removed, of course, peace would be assured.

By the 1st century, the Jewish people had many factions each with their own ideas of how deliverance would come. When King Herod, a ruler appointed by Rome but himself a practising Jew, was visited by the Magi and told a king of the Jews had been born he immediately called upon the priests and scholars. He asked them to confirm the city prophesied for the birth for the Messiah. Herod was so intimidated by the prospect of a challenger to his rule, he ordered the massacre of all male babies under two years old.[1] He would rather be the ruler-of-sorts under Roman jurisdiction than have a messiah come to bring permanent peace. His actions show, however, that despite all the connotations in the Hebrew language for peace meaning restoration, the only 'peace without end' the Israelites seemed to be able to imagine was the absence of domination.

Looking back from here in the 21st century, we can see how the fulfilment of the restoration and reconciliation prophecies wasn't what the Israelites expected. The peace the Messiah brought was not a political or earthly peace nor was it a re-marking of land territory. The peace without end wasn't something they could write about in history annals, like the recording of a dynasty.

The peace brought by the Messiah was far bigger than a change in local ruler, and far more wide-reaching. The peace caused dramatic changes in

---

1   Matthew 2:1-17

individuals and ultimately changed the whole world. But the Prince of Peace was nothing like they imagined.

A narrow view of peace (or any other concept) doesn't limit God but it might mean we don't notice the work God is doing or we get frustrated when things don't turn out how we expect. We can't join in with the work God is doing if we aren't aware of it happening.

When you pray for help or rescue, how easy do you find it to steer away from telling God how he should do it?

Is it easier to see possible ways God is working in the lives of others than in our own lives?

Have you ever failed to notice when God was at work in your life?

Prayer
Father God, We ask you open our minds to understand ways you work in our world today. Help us see where you are and how we can join in. Amen.

And there were shepherds living out in the fields nearby, keeping watch over their flocks at night. An angel of the Lord appeared to them, and the glory of the Lord shone around them, and they were terrified. But the angel said to them, "Do not be afraid. I bring you good news that will cause great joy for all the people. Today in the town of David a Saviour has been born to you; he is the Messiah, the Lord. This will be a sign to you: You will find a baby wrapped in cloths and lying in a manger."
Suddenly a great company of the heavenly host appeared with the angel, praising God and saying, "Glory to God in the highest heaven, and on earth peace to those on whom his favour rests." When the angels had left them and gone into heaven, the shepherds said to one another, "Let's go to Bethlehem and see this thing that has happened, which the Lord has told us about."

LUKE 2:8-15

Day 3

Peace arrives

Mary delivers the baby, wraps him in cloths and lays him down in an animal's feeding trough. Around the same time, an angel appears to a group of shepherds guarding their animals out on the hillside. The text says the glory of the Lord shone all around them. Even the smallest flame looks dramatic when shining in the darkness and even the slimmest crack in the curtains at night can prevent us from sleep, so we should have no difficulty imagining the extent of the brightness exhibited here. The countryside around the shepherds lights up dramatically and inexplicably. The shepherds see the angel and hear his message. The Messiah had been born. The saviour that the Jewish people had been told to expect for generations had arrived. The shepherds aren't told the baby's name but only where to find him and how he will be wrapped. It was like a first-century scavenger hunt.

If the shepherds ever doubted what they first heard, they likely had no time to acknowledge it for straight-away a host of angels appeared. This crowd acknowledged and declared the glory of God, singing out the assurance of the coming of peace on earth. It's incongruous to consider how unpeaceful this announcement of peace likely was. Even good news can be shocking when we aren't expecting change.

Before the angels turned up, the shepherds probably considered they were experiencing a kind of peace on that hillside: the sheep were penned safely away, the fire was built, the people familiar, the food the same as always, the conversation predictable.

We can create and experience peace by following well-practiced routines and by removing things we know to be annoying. If we're honest, we know our rituals create only temporary and shallow peace. When something happens to disrupt our habits or customs, our peace is disrupted also. We can build our peace on daily routines, interactions, or indulgences, but then any shift

THE KIND OF PEACE WE CREATE FOR OURSELVES IS MERELY A LULL IN THE DISORDER

in those creates unrest. Suddenly our peace is gone. The kind of peace we create for ourselves is merely a lull in the disorder—it is quietness not necessarily shalom.

Many families would have arrived in Bethlehem for the census and we know the inn was full. The normal peace of Bethlehem had been interrupted and doubtless everyone was looking forward to the return of their regular peace and quiet. Conversely, the shepherds' peace was interrupted to alert them of the arrival of a better peace. The Messiah, the prince of peace, is born at last. The shepherds went directly into Bethlehem leaving their hillside in order to find this saviour baby.

Mary's quiet was no doubt disrupted by the arrival of the shepherd visitors. While her earthly peace may have been interrupted, the effect of their visit may have given her a long-lasting reassurance that her baby was indeed the Messiah. Quietness, reassurance, calmness, stillness: these are all words we use synonymously with the word peace, but it is not the peace this baby was to bring.

What are some ways you try to create earthly peace for yourself?

In what ways do you confuse the transient peace we can create ourselves with the peace that Jesus offers?

Have you ever been in a situation where you've traded lasting peace for something more temporary?

Prayer
Father God, Show me where I've looked for peace in the wrong places and help me instead find it in you. Amen.

Peace I leave with you; my peace I give you. I do not give to you as the world gives. Do not let your hearts be troubled and do not be afraid."

JOHN 14:27

Day 4

Peace has a source

True peace is not a product of the right set of external circumstances nor does it come from our own nature. We humans are naturally inclined to argue and look to our own interests. We are not even persuaded to the right-here-right-now kind of peace unless it so happens that we are getting exactly what we want, how we want it and when we expected it.

When Elizabeth interrupted the naming ceremony to prevent her son being named after Zechariah, everyone jumped in to argue before turning to Zechariah himself to settle things. His action of writing on the tablet 'His name is John' brought peace to the commotion and also miraculously restored (brought wholeness, *shalom*) to his vocal abilities. His public act of obedience to God marked the end of the most noticeable indicator of his visitation by the angel in the temple.

With his new-found voice, Zechariah prophecies that the coming of the Messiah will allow God's people to serve him without fear, in holiness and righteousness all their days. He describes true peace. He tells the listeners that his son will prepare the people for the Lord and that Jesus will 'guide our feet into the path of peace.'[1] I like how he includes himself when he talks about being guided. Despite his expert knowledge of the scriptures and his whole life's work in service to God at the temple, he was humble enough to know he needed to be led.

Zechariah joyfully declares that there is a path of peace and it's needed by us all. We all need Jesus. Jesus isn't an add-on or an 'in case of an emergency button'. We can't do life wholeheartedly without relying entirely on his strength and his leading. We don't graduate from needing Jesus in our lives. God's tender mercy reveals the path to peace which is the path to wholeness.

Years later, prompted by the Holy Spirit and as a fulfilment of prophecies from Malachi and Isaiah, the adult John preached in the wilderness around the Jordan area telling all who would hear that the Messiah was coming.[2] Soon after, John baptised Jesus before he began his public ministry and called him 'the Lamb of God who takes away the sin of the world!'[3] Jesus taking away the sin of the world was the path of peace Zechariah spoke about.

John and Jesus both taught about the path to peace and reconciliation, but also made it clear we are never pressured to take it. Relationships with Christ-followers, messages from speakers, music and literature and art can all lead us to find where peace begins, but ultimately, it is our choice whether we walk towards it once we see it.

Following Jesus' death, one of his disciples, Peter, is invited to visit a household to talk about the events surrounding Jesus life and

---

1   Luke 1:79
2   Luke 3:3
3   John 1:29

resurrection. Peter recaps how what he saw and heard and goes on to explain the forgiveness of sins. Peter calls it 'the good news of peace through Jesus Christ.'[4] The reason peace through Jesus was good news was that now God accepted everyone who put their faith in him. Jesus bought peace from striving to be good enough for our Holy God, not quietness and the absence of discord. This peace wholly brought by Jesus is the completeness we experience as we are fully accepted as blameless by God. When we realise we are seen as blameless no matter what we've done then we can fully appreciate the good news of peace.

Can you recall how you found 'the path of peace' (that is, recognising Jesus as someone who could reconcile you to a relationship with God)?

Did someone talk to you about Jesus? Or was it something you read or something you heard?

Prayer
God, Thank you for the ways you show us the path of peace. Help us to walk it. Amen.

4   Acts 10:36-43

Do not be anxious about anything, but in every situation, by prayer and petition, with thanksgiving, present your requests to God. And the peace of God, which transcends all understanding, will guard your hearts and your minds in Christ Jesus.

PHILIPPIANS 4:6-7

Day 5

Remarkable Peace

If we define peace only as a feeling, today's verse can seem very confusing. I'm not sure anyone in the world ever has stopped feeling anxious by being told not to feel anxious. Today's verse tells us that our peace is not dependent on our circumstances but comes from God. God's peace can stand guard of our mind to prevent truths we know leaking out or falsehoods sneaking in. Our feelings cannot always be trusted. We can have a feeling of peace about something that turned out to be a disaster, or likewise an unpeaceful, disturbing feeling for no reason whatsoever.

When we see someone keep calm and respond peacefully when their circumstances would otherwise induce agitation we notice. It's noticeable perhaps because it's rare. When bad things happen we normally respond emotionally, even dramatically. Media news outlets push us stories of people 'just like us' who acted passionately following betrayal or loss. Peter, a disciple of Jesus, got outraged when Jesus was arrested in the garden of Gethsemane and cut the ear off a soldier. Responding dramatically to stress and adverse events isn't new.

Depending on what our peace is based on, like joy, peace as a feeling can coexist with other emotions. Peter's peace was based on how he thought things should happen (which was Jesus staying alive and keeping on teaching them all, not being arrested and not being taken off for trial). If Peter's peace stood on the fundamental belief that God was in control and Jesus was living obediently to God's will, perhaps he wouldn't have acted so rashly. That kind of peace would surely have guarded his mind and helped him not react aggressively in fear.

When we are faced with circumstances that might stir up all manner of emotions or reactions, we can choose how we behave. We can choose to react with peace. Like joy that we discussed last week, peace is an outcome of the working of the Holy Spirit in our lives. While peace (and joy and the others) are fruit of the Holy Spirit, we still need to walk that way. We must choose to allow the visible work of the Holy Spirit.

THE PEACE OF GOD CAN GUARD OUR MIND AS IT REMINDS US WHERE OUR HOPE AND OUR SECURITY ARE TRULY FOUND

If we only think of peace as the absence of conflict, then whenever circumstances are challenging or unpleasant we will consider ourselves in hardship. Thinking of ourselves in hardship can cause us to respond to our circumstances from a position of perceived injustice.

The peace of God can guard our mind as it reminds us where our hope and our security are truly found.

146

Our security is not the absence of suffering. In this world we will have trouble and hardship. We won't always get what we want or even what we think we need. Our security is not found in any calm earthly circumstance. While there is evil in the world, we will have war and unfairness and poverty and disease. And this will remain until Jesus comes again (which he will).

In the presence of fretfulness, we can allow peace to guard our hearts and our minds to ensure we respond from a place of security. Our peace comes from knowing who we are (God's dearly loved children[1]), knowing where we will go when we leave this earth (heaven to be with God[2]) and knowing we have everything we need for life[3].

Personal note: If you experience the kind of anxiety that affects how you live your life and you are not currently talking to a professional about it, I would encourage you to reach out for help. If you take medication or are involved in therapy of any kind to help manage your anxiety, please do not stop your treatment as a result of this reading. The professionals who treat you know you and your history; I am just a girl who writes things.

1   Ephesians 5:1
2   John 14:1-3
3   2 Peter 1:3

Can you think of a time
where someone reacted in
peace when it might be more
expected that they would be
agitated?

Why do you think stories of
people acting peacefully when
they could act in anger or
revenge are surprising to us?

Do you think stories of
incidents like this are rare
or just not reported in the
media?

Prayer
Father God, We ask for your peace
to guard our minds. Each day there
are so many ways we can be discouraged
and afraid and confused, so we ask for your
peace that is beyond human understanding to calm us. Amen.

IMITATE GOD, THEREFORE, IN EVERYTHING YOU DO, BECAUSE YOU ARE HIS DEAR CHILDREN

EPHESIANS 5:1 NLT

DON'T LET YOUR HEARTS BE TROUBLED. TRUST IN GOD, AND TRUST ALSO IN ME. THERE IS MORE THAN ENOUGH ROOM IN MY FATHER'S HOME. IF THIS WERE NOT SO, WOULD I HAVE TOLD YOU THAT I AM GOING TO PREPARE A PLACE FOR YOU? WHEN EVERYTHING IS READY, I WILL COME AND GET YOU, SO THAT YOU WILL ALWAYS BE WITH ME WHERE I AM.

JOHN 14:1-3 NLT

EVERYTHING WE COULD EVER NEED FOR LIFE AND GODLINESS HAS ALREADY BEEN DEPOSITED IN US BY HIS DIVINE POWER

2 PETER 1:3 TPT

Be completely humble and gentle; be patient,
bearing with one another in love.
Make every effort to keep the unity of the Spirit
through the bond of peace.

EPHESIANS 4:2-3

For God was pleased to have all his fullness dwell
in him, and through him to reconcile to himself
all things, whether things on earth or things in
heaven, by making peace through his blood,
shed on the cross.

COLOSSIANS 1:19-20

Day 6

Peacemakers for life

Reading about Jesus and how he ministered with the disciples, his life doesn't strike me as peaceful. At least not by our generally earthly definition. Jesus was itinerant with no permanent home to return to each night, he moved around a lot. Wherever he went there were misunderstandings, sometimes conflict, and people demanded much of him. There were some towns Jesus temporarily avoided as the animosity there was so great, and of course, he was eventually subjected to an unfair trial before he was brutally executed.

In the sense that peace is the absence of political or social conflict, or even that peace means interpersonal or family harmony, Jesus' life doesn't seem to fit with that definition. Jesus talked about how the world hated him. The way the world treated him was no surprise to him and he said that we can expect to be hated sometimes too.[1] Yet, Jesus was secure in his purpose, secure in his

---

1   John 15:17-20

status as God's son, secure in where he would ultimately end up, and totally secure in what resources were available to him to fulfil his purpose and in so doing bring God glory.

During the sermon on the mount, Jesus said that God blesses those who work for peace. He is more famously quoted 'blessed are the peacemakers.'[2]

Peacemakers work to create peace by attempting to reconcile things and people who are at odds with one another. Often, reconciling people requires changes in mindset and processes. Change can feel like a disruption to our peace. A group who perceives a disruption in their future but who are currently quite content with their situation might employ peacekeeping tactics. Peacekeepers are not the same as peacemakers. Peacekeepers strive to keep peace at any cost. Peacemakers might initiate change or disruption because they see how changes in ways of doing will benefit society. Peacekeepers have no desire for new ways of doing things because the ways they've always been done are perceived to be good enough.

Becoming people of peace doesn't mean we stay out of everything and never suggest changes. As Jesus ministered on earth he asked questions of people which sometimes made them uncomfortable. Jesus did this with the goal that those who heard might know greater truths than those they might otherwise consider. One rich young ruler we read about 'goes away feeling sad' after Jesus talks to him about his life.[3] Perhaps not everything we say will bring immediate happiness, but it might bring ultimate wholeness.

---

2 Matthew 5:9
3 Mark 10:22

We face this choice: to let the peace of Christ rule or to let something else rule.

Of course, Jesus was much better at being loving and kind than we are. When Jesus spoke the truth he was never rude. In his letter to the Colossians Paul tells believers to 'let the peace of Christ rule in your hearts'.[4] Letting the peace of Christ rule in our hearts will mean we can act in love with forgiveness and gentleness and compassion. Do we make sure our actions conform to what rules us, or do we choose to react based on what's happening in our circumstances? Paul writes much in many of his letters about unity among believers. He implores us to 'make every effort to do what leads to peace.'[5] We shouldn't be stirring things up for no reason. Creating discord goes against what else Paul says in the same letter 'so far as it depends on you, live peaceably with all.'[6]

WE WILL NOT HAVE PEACE AS WE LIKE TO DEFINE IT UNTIL JESUS RETURNS TO REIGN ON EARTH

We will not have peace as we like to define it until Jesus returns and reigns on earth. Until that time, we can practice being peacemakers and we can act peacefully. We can choose to remember from where our peace and our wholeness comes whenever we feel broken-hearted or fretful. We can be aware how our behaviour affects others so that when we find ourselves in strife or personal conflict, we can be quick to be gentle, quick to forgive, and quick to remove barriers that prevent reconciliation.

---

4 Colossians 3:15
5 Romans 14:19
6 Romans 12:18

Have you experienced the
difference between
peacemakers and peacekeepers?

In what ways do you think
Christians contribute to conflict
rather than show peace?

Do you think it possible to be love
someone and tell them the path there
are on will not lead to lasting peace?

Prayer
Heavenly Father, Forgive me for the
times when I've not acted peacefully. Show
me where I can be a peacemaker and give me
the courage to speak out. Amen.

For God so loved the world that he gave his one and only Son, that whoever believes in him shall not perish but have eternal life. For God did not send his Son into the world to condemn the world, but to save the world through him.

JOHN 3:16-17

Day 7

It's a privilege to have peace with God

Today is our last day of this four-week look at the Christmas story through the lens of hope, faith, joy and peace.

The birth of Jesus was miraculous and amazing. His birth brought joy to many at the time as their hope was realised and their faith strengthened. When Jesus came to earth he came not to stay a baby but to grow into a man who would accomplish God's purpose on earth. That purpose was to atone for our sin and restore the broken relationship between us and God. This was God's plan from before the beginning of time and was unachievable by anyone other than the perfect son of God.

One of Jesus' closest friends, the apostle called John (not John the Baptiser, a different John) compiled an account of Jesus' life to remind us of the very deep love God has for all humankind. God sent his only son into the world in order that we might be given eternal life. John tells us directly that it was God's very great love for us that caused him to make this sacrifice as the only way to solve the problem of our separation and sin.

Before the fall, before when sin entered the world, humankind walked with God in peace. We were secure in the knowledge that God was trustworthy and perfect, and that he loved us. Since then, we've struggled against him, worried whether he is good and doubted his intentions. Our sinful nature first created when sin entered the world makes a barrier to our closeness with God as our sinfulness contrasts with his holiness.

Yet, from the ancient past when God selected his chosen people he created events to demonstrate his character and show his boundless love.

Right from the beginning and despite our natural sinful natures God loved us but, without Jesus, our lives would be lived separated from God and our actions punishable by death. Death was the price of our sin.

So, Jesus died in our place.

He died so we could live.

Without what Jesus did, our lives would end without any experience of being with God.

When we define peace as wholeness it means we can grasp how the process of peace is one of reconciliation. Jesus came so we could have peace, not just the feeling that everything will be alright one day (which it will) but a peace between us and God so that we can again come into communion with him. This peace means we can be seen without blemish, as entirely perfect, as completely blameless. We are now forever forgiven children of God.

THIS PEACE MEANS WE CAN BE SEEN WITHOUT BLEMISH, AS ENTIRELY PERFECT, AS COMPLETELY BLAMELESS. WE ARE NOW FOREVER FORGIVEN CHILDREN OF GOD

We can read the story of Jesus' birth, and the faith of Mary and Joseph, the joy of Zechariah and Elizabeth, the shepherds, and Simeon in the temple, and we can share in their thrilled amazement. We know so much more completely now than they did then. We can see the events of these months as the starting point for something so revolutionary in our relationship with God. Humanity's broken relationship would be wonderfully and permanently restored. Through the infant Jesus in the manger growing up to be the incredible man and perfect lamb we are given peace— peace from the impossible striving to please God and peace from the shame of our mistakes and peace from the breach between God and man.

Jesus' life, death and resurrection reconciled all things in heaven and on earth, and this was the perfect peace that was prophesied and intended all along.

> *Justified through faith we have peace with God through Jesus Christ.*
> ROMANS 5:1

It's a privilege that we can all now have peace with God.

What does peace with God
mean to you?

Have you ever considered that
peace with God is a privilege,
something we didn't earn?

Have you ever considered Jesus'
adult life and eventual death to
be part of the Christmas story?

If you pray this prayer on the opposite page, I'd love to hear about it.
You can let me know through my website (see the copyright page). You
might also look for a Bible-believing church near you.
Meeting other Christ-followers can help us in our faith journey, and
also we get to share in one-another's joy!

What to do if you would like this peace with God...

When someone hears the message of hope and peace in God through Jesus, a friend or the Christ-follower they are with often helps them in what's called 'the sinners prayer.'

Put simply, it's a phrase for a phrase used to describe that we want to accept we are a sinner and ask God for forgiveness and demonstrate that we believe in the saving power of Jesus' death and resurrection. There is a verse in the book of Romans in the Bible that says 'If you declare with your mouth, "Jesus is Lord," and believe in your heart that God raised him from the dead, you will be saved. For it is with your heart that you believe and are justified, and it is with your mouth that you profess your faith and are saved.'[1]

If that's what you would like to do, then I've written a prayer for you below because I can't be with you in person. These words aren't special words, but it doesn't really matter what exact words you say because the saving power comes from Jesus not from a special sequence of words.

Heavenly Father,
I realise that I am a sinner and I cannot save myself. Forgive me of my sins. I believe that Jesus died for and rose again and that is all that is necessary for me to be called your child and seen by you as blameless. Today I give you my trust and declare I want to live for you. Fill me with your Spirit so I can know you and follow you for the rest of my life. Thank you for hearing my prayer. Amen

Just think—Heaven is rejoicing over you!

If this is all you have time for this week...

PEACE OR QUIET Peace is not the same as quiet. The kinds of peace we imagine from Christmas cards, advertising and movies are temporary and easily interrupted. Peace as defined in the Bible, or *shalom* as it's called in Ancient Hebrew, is completeness, safety and wholeness. In a world that's fractured by conflict and broken by disease it's perhaps easy to see how safety and wholeness are desirable.

SEPARATION, THE PRICE OF SIN & THE GIFT OF LIFE Our own natures bring us into conflict with one-another and, more devastatingly, separate us from God. God is entirely complete and sufficient, all knowing and all powerful, unchanging, forever present and always everywhere. As God is holy and perfect, so our sinful nature separates us from his holiness and perfection. Even worse, there is a required punishment for our sin—death. Rather than leave us in such a dire situation, God's great love made a way for us to be become completely acceptable and exempt from punishment. God's son Jesus saved us from what our sin deserved.

RELATIONSHIP, NOT RULES Jesus didn't bring us a list of list of rules to follow but said we could draw near to him and talk to him like a friend. Jesus didn't introduce a lifestyle blueprint of external behaviours to adopt but instead said we could call ourselves God's children. Jesus didn't get us a work-plan but said we were entirely loved just as we were. Jesus himself was the gift that wiped away our punishment and set us up for a relationship with God.

162

GOD'S PLAN FROM THE START God's plan from before the beginning of time ensured we could be reconciled. The punishment we deserved because of our sin, his son Jesus came to earth to take care in our place. Jesus died in our place. Jesus' death means our punishment is paid in full and we can stand blameless before God, as the dearly loved children we have always been.

PEACE IN EVERY WAY Christmas is when we recall how Jesus' birth started the events that brought about our peace with God and the ability to live on earth in peace. We have insight from Jesus and his apostles to show us how to live full lives in harmony with one another. We have the victory of Jesus' resurrection to reassure us of our own resurrection after we die and a witness to the all-surpassing power of God. We have inside us peace that transcends human understanding to equip us in every way to perseverance and live free, abundant lives on earth.

WE CAN CHOOSE PEACE By choosing to allow Jesus to be our peace, to declare he is Lord and believe he rose from the dead, we are saved, made whole, completely at peace with God, and therefore assured of our place with him forever.

It's a privilege to be reconciled with God

Printed in Great Britain
by Amazon

69938965R00098